Finding North in Your Life

A Path to Spiritual Awareness

Thomas Gladstone

with
Jeff B. Miller

ISBN (eBook): 978-1-967120-28-4

ISBN (Paperback): 978-1-967120-29-1

ISBN (Hardcover): 978-1-967120-30-7

Cover by Tia Rigsby.

Published by Indie Christian Book in Bloomington, Illinois, U.S.A.

www.indiechristianbook.com

Contents

Foreword

I have known Tom Gladstone and his wonderful wife Tami for more than four decades. We met when I was hired to the staff of Young Life in Fairfax, Virginia, and the Gladstones were part of the hosting committee. Tom is a man of profound character with a deep love for God, and a deep commitment to the wide swath of relationships in his and Tami's lives. Tom exemplifies Jesus' Great Command: to love God with all our heart, mind, soul and strength, and to love our neighbor as ourselves.

Tom and I have collaborated on several initiatives with Young Life —helping launch our middle school ministry, beginning our alumni program, and building bridges to the Catholic Church, just to name a few. I count Tom and Tami as essential partners in my current focus to help Young Life and churches work together to reach unchurched teens and their families. There is great promise ahead in this endeavor!

Tom's lifelong fascination with maps and his expertise as a naval cartographer has given him a perspective from which we can all glean for navigating our way through life. Tom's claim is true: "When we lose our orientation in life, what we really need is not a new destination, but a return to True North."

I share Tom's conviction that life works as it was intended only when we are oriented to True North. If we take our eyes off of our Creator and try to navigate ourselves, we are bound to hit obstacles, many of which can derail us from the life of thriving we seek.

Foreword

We each have a unique map for how we experience God and discover His purposes. I'm thankful I was introduced to a personal relationship with Jesus in my teens that continues to grow today. There is more of Jesus for us to get to know at every compass point. I urge us to lean into what this seasoned navigator has to say. I guarantee you will know yourself and your Lord better as a result of reading this book.

Happy Navigating!

Rick Beckwith

Church Collaborations, Young Life

Introduction

This book is not about me.

Although you'll learn a great deal about my life along the way, this book is really about you, the reader. It's about hope. It's about prayer. It's about how God shows up in the middle of our afflictions and redirects us toward True North.

My prayer is that, as you read, you'll discover God's fingerprints on your own story. Perhaps you'll recognize Him in moments you'd forgotten, or in seasons when you thought you were alone. Perhaps you'll realize that the very disorientation you feel today is His invitation to recalibrate your compass and look up.

Hope, affliction, and prayer. At first glance, they may sound like three unrelated words. Yet Romans 12:12 reminds us: "Be _joyful_ in hope, _patient_ in affliction, _faithful_ in prayer" (NIV, emphasis added). These three are divinely intertwined. Hope looks forward to God's promises. Affliction presses us to let go of our self-sufficiency and trust Him. Prayer ties the two together, becoming the lifeline that steadies us when we can't see the way.

Over the years, I've learned that prayer isn't complicated; it is simply conversation. Sometimes whispered in the dark, sometimes shouted in frustration, sometimes groaned through tears. But always powerful. Always heard. Always the bridge between our present disorientation and God's steady presence.

You'll also notice another thread woven throughout this book:

maps. I began my career as a cartographer in the U.S. Air Force, making maps long before satellites and computers took over. I was fascinated by the way lines and contours could orient a traveler, how one mark in the right place could change everything about the journey. In those years, I came to understand a simple truth: a map is only useful if it's oriented to True North. Without that, you can have all the details in the world and still end up lost.

That same truth applies to life. The Bible is our roadmap. God Himself is our North Star. And through the Spirit's quiet guidance, we can reorient ourselves when storms, distractions, or wrong assumptions pull us off course.

This is a Christ-centered book. Everything in it flows from my faith in Jesus Christ, who has been my True North through cancer, career, family, and failures. But I've written it in the hope that even those who don't yet share that faith, especially my fellow veterans who know what it feels like to navigate hostile terrain, will find encouragement here. Because all of us, sooner or later, lose our bearings. And all of us need to find our way home.

So consider this an invitation. Not to learn more about me, but to take another look at your own journey. To search for God's direction. To rediscover hope. To have patience with His timing. And through prayer, to hear His call again, or perhaps for the very first time.

Part One

Lost Without a Map

Chapter 1

First Things First

When Life Loses Direction

 To fall in love with God is the greatest romance; to seek him the greatest adventure; to find him, the greatest human achievement.

— St. Augustine

 Be joyful in hope, patient in affliction, faithful in prayer.

— Romans 12:12 NIV

I never expected pancreatic cancer to be the thing that reoriented my life.

It began as something small. A dull ache in my side. A few inconclusive tests. Some off-kilter numbers. My doctor suspected a gallstone, maybe a bile duct blockage. But then came the words that upended everything: tumor, malignant, surgery.

What followed was an eleven-hour Whipple procedure, one of the most complicated surgeries in modern medicine. They removed the head of my pancreas, part of my stomach, my duodenum, and an inflamed gallbladder that, according to the surgeon, looked like a rock. The pathology report showed that several lymph nodes had tested positive for cancerous cells. The cancer wasn't just in one place. It had spread. Chemo was next.

I've lived a long, full life. I've been a husband, a father, grandfather, great-grandfather, an Air Force officer, a cartographer, a consultant, a friend. I've known purpose. I've known movement. But sitting in that sterile hospital room, hearing the words "we'll need to start chemotherapy soon," I felt the ground shift underneath me.

My unsteadiness wasn't fear or trepidation; it was disorientation. I wasn't sure where my life was anymore. After all, even at eighty-one years old, my overall health has been good. However, through the cancer journey, I started thinking about how I have navigated through my life and the ways God has pulled me through many ups and downs as my True North. How did I orient my life against the True North? I started thinking about maps, which have been inspirational in my life, and how the map to find God has been there all along, even though I did not always recognize Him.

We've All Been There

Maybe you haven't faced cancer, but you've surely felt disoriented.

That disorientation could have come from the loss of a job or a marriage, a diagnosis or a disappointment, a betrayal or just a slow fading of purpose. Sometimes everything looks fine on the surface, but inside, you feel like you've lost your way. You wake up one day and realize you've been navigating by instinct, momentum, or emotion, and somewhere along the line, you drifted off course.

The landscape around you no longer makes sense. The old maps don't work. The goals that once motivated you now feel hollow. The relationships that used to anchor you may have shifted or disappeared. You might be succeeding by every external measure. You have a good job, nice house, functioning routines, but internally, something fundamental feels misaligned.

You're not broken. You're not failing. You're simply lost.

Here's what I've learned: Being lost isn't the problem. Refusing to admit it is.

Because when we lose our orientation in life, what we really need is not a new destination, but a return to True North. We don't need another self-help strategy or a five-step plan to reinvent ourselves. We need to stop, look up, and remember what we're here for in the first place.

That feeling of disorientation, that uncomfortable awareness that something is off, isn't failure. It's the invitation to recalibrate. To become honest. To remember who you are beneath all the noise, expectations, and survival strategies you've built up over the years.

This book is for anyone who's ever felt that way. Which means it's for all of us.

Rediscovering the Map

As a boy, I was obsessed with maps. On long family road trips, I would ride with one unfolded across my lap, tracing the highways with my finger, connecting our journey over rivers and through cities, trying to picture what lay ahead. Later, I made maps professionally as a cartographer in the Air Force—back when everything was still done by hand.

The first thing you learn in mapmaking is this: If True North isn't correctly marked at the top, nothing else works. It doesn't matter how accurate the roads are or how detailed the terrain. If the orientation is off, you'll stay or soon become lost.

Many of us are lost today, not because we're on the wrong road, but because we've lost our sense of what direction is actually up.

When we rely on instincts, old beliefs, or someone else's outdated version of our story without understanding where North is, we drift. Without North, we panic. Without North, we try to fix the map instead of turning it in the right direction.

The North Star Still Shines

The North Star, Polaris, sits nearly directly above the Earth's North Pole. It doesn't appear to move. Every other star shifts and spins across the night sky, tracing arcs from horizon to horizon as the Earth rotates beneath them. But because Polaris lies almost perfectly aligned with Earth's rotational axis, it remains nearly stationary in the northern sky while everything else wheels around it.

For centuries, travelers across oceans and deserts could find their way by it. Sailors navigating vast, featureless seas. Merchants crossing trackless deserts. Refugees fleeing persecution in the dead of night. They all looked up, found that single unwavering point of light, and knew which way was north. If they could see the North Star, they could orient themselves. They could chart a course. They could find their way home.

It isn't the brightest star in the sky, not even close. But its value isn't in its brilliance. It's in its constant state *from our perspective*. It's trustworthy precisely because, from where we stand on Earth, it doesn't seem to change. No matter what season, no matter what storm, no matter how far you've wandered, Polaris is there, appearing in the same place, offering the same silent guidance.

God is like that—but even more so.

Because while Polaris only *appears* fixed due to our position relative to it, God truly is unchanging, even when everything around you moves. When your health fails, when your finances spiral, when relationships fracture, when the ground beneath you shifts, God doesn't move. His position is absolute. His presence is steady. His character is unchanging.

 Jesus Christ is the same yesterday and today and forever.

— Hebrews 13:8

He is not subject to our circumstances. He is not dependent on our understanding or our perspective. He doesn't shift with our moods or fade with our doubt. When we're confused, He's clear. When we're unsteady, He's solid. When we feel like everything is spinning out of control, He remains exactly where He's always been, not just appearing steady from our limited viewpoint, but actually, eternally, unchangeable.

When we lose our way, the problem isn't that God disappears. It's that we lose sight of Him. Clouds roll in—pain, fear, distraction, disappointment—and we forget where to look. Or worse, we look at the wrong things altogether: our plans, our accomplishments, other people's approval, our own ability to hold it together. And those things, no matter how good they are, move. They shift. They fail. They were never meant to be our True North.

But when we lift our eyes back to Him, when we stop, breathe, and remember who God is, we find our orientation again. Not because our circumstances have changed, but because we've remembered what's unchanging.

6

Biblical Compass Points

This sense of being lost isn't new.

The Israelites, after being miraculously freed from slavery, wandered in the wilderness and cried out to return to Egypt when the path got hard (Numbers 14). They had seen the presence of God in fire and a cloud. They had tasted manna. But when the path stretched longer than expected, they doubted.

Or consider Paul, then Saul, confidently marching on the road to Damascus, utterly convinced he was right...until he was blinded and knocked to the ground. Only in the darkness did he discover he'd been walking the wrong way (Acts 9).

Isaiah writes it plainly: "All we like sheep have gone astray; we have turned—every one—to his own way" (Isaiah 53:6).

Wandering isn't the exception. It's the condition of being human.

When the Map is Wrong

Here's a strange but true story.

For over 200 years, many European maps showed California as an island. It started in the early 1600s when a Spanish explorer misinterpreted the geography of the Baja Peninsula and the Gulf of California. Perhaps he sailed up the gulf, saw land on both sides, and assumed he'd found a strait separating California from the mainland. Or maybe the error came from a corrupted report, a mistranslation, or simply wishful thinking, the desire to discover something dramatic and new.

Whatever the cause, the mistake stuck. Cartographers copied it from map to map. Explorers consulted those maps and sailed in search of waterways that didn't exist. Ship captains charted courses based on false landmarks. Investors funded expeditions to navigate around an island that was actually a peninsula firmly attached to the continent.

The error persisted for generations, not because no one questioned it, but because the maps had authority. They were beautifully drawn, widely distributed, stamped with official seals. They looked trustworthy. And once an error becomes established, it takes extraordinary effort to correct it. People who actually sailed along the California coast and saw with their own eyes that it was connected to the mainland were dismissed. "The maps say otherwise," they were told.

It wasn't until the early 1700s, after decades of contradictory evidence piled up, that cartographers finally corrected the mistake. California was not, and never had been, an island.

But by then, countless ships had wasted time, money, and lives searching for passages that weren't there, all because someone, somewhere, got their bearings wrong, and everyone else trusted the map more than reality.

You see where this is going.

We all have inherited maps, pointing to success, to God, to direction in relationships, to wisdom about ourselves. Sometimes these maps are just...wrong.

Maybe you were taught that being in control is the key to safety. Or that achievement leads to meaning. Or that being good allows you to avoid pain.

But those aren't maps, they're myths.

God isn't an idea we invent. He's a Presence we discover.

And discovering Him requires something many of us avoid: reflection.

You: Start Here

This book is an invitation, not to religion or rigidity, but to reorientation.

It's a call to stop spinning, stop guessing, and look up. To find, maybe for the first time in a long time, that the North Star still shines.

Wherever you are, at a crossroads, in a fog, or adrift on open water, you can start again. You don't have to see the whole path. You just need to find North.

You'll find that God is still there.

He's not panicking. He's not lost. And He hasn't forgotten you.

Navigation Callout: The Compass That Pointed South

In the 1800s, iron shipbuilding revolutionized naval travel, but created an unexpected problem. The massive iron hulls interfered with magnetic compasses, causing them to point in the wrong direction. Captains who trusted their instruments without correction sailed confidently toward disaster.

The solution wasn't to abandon the compass. It was to understand the interference and compensate for it. Naval officers developed "deviation cards" showing how much the ship's structure pulled the needle off course. Once they knew the distortion, they could navigate accurately again.

Our lives are the same way. We all have internal "magnetic interference": fears, wounds, pride, past failures, cultural pressure that pulls our sense of direction off true. We think we're heading north when we're actually drifting east.

Finding True North isn't just about looking up at God. It's also about honest self-examination: What's pulling my compass off course? What am I trusting that's distorting my direction?

Recalibration requires both humility and courage, the humility to admit when something inside us is off, and the courage to make the adjustment.

Reflection and Application

1. Where in your life do you feel most disoriented right now?
2. Have you been navigating with a clear sense of True North, or just reacting?
3. What inherited "maps" or beliefs might be misleading you?
4. What would it mean to stop, look up, and find North again?

A Prayer for Orientation

God, I confess that I've been moving without direction. I've trusted instincts, old habits, and secondhand maps. But I want to find You, my True North. Help me see through the fog. Help me hear Your quiet voice. I don't need the whole plan, I just want to find You again. Amen.

Chapter 2

The Call to Find Your Way

 "Come, follow me," Jesus said, "and I will send you out to fish for people."

— Matthew 4:19 NIV

In 1853, a sickly twenty-year-old college dropout lay in bed, convinced he was dying. He'd failed at West Point, failed in business, and now his body was failing him. Wracked with what doctors called "consumption," he could barely walk across a room without gasping for breath.

Something strange happened during those bedridden months. Theodore Roosevelt, for that's who this young man was, heard a call. Not a voice from heaven, but a conviction that rose from somewhere deep inside: He would not let weakness define him. He would build his body as deliberately as other men built houses.

"I'll make my body," he declared to his father. And he did. Through what he called "the strenuous life," that sickly boy transformed himself into a force of nature, boxer, rancher, explorer, soldier, and eventually President of the United States.

Here's what Roosevelt understood that many miss: The call to transformation rarely comes when we're strong. It comes when we're weak, lost, and out of options. It comes when we finally admit we can't keep drifting.

A Greater Call

Roosevelt's declaration was powerful. It transformed his life and shaped a nation. But the call I want to tell you about goes deeper than physical transformation or worldly achievement. It's the call to spiritual navigation, to finding your True North in God Himself.

This is the call that echoes through Scripture and through the ages: "Come, follow me." It's not just a call to better yourself or achieve your potential. It's a call to discover why you exist, where you're meant to go, and Who is calling you there.

The call says: "There's another way to live, not just successfully, but purposefully. Not just achieving, but victoriously arriving at the destination I've planned for you. Will you take this way of purpose?"

What If You Could Always Know Which Way to Go?

Some might desire to always know what path to take and what choices to make. Not in the vague, fortune-cookie sense, but a true, steady direction. That's a calling. What if you had a map that could show you such a way? This type of purpose would be an assurance that your steps matter, your choices are aligned, and your life is headed somewhere that means something eternal.

The truth is this type of calling is available to everyone.

However, for a long time, I didn't have that.

Drifting Without a Compass

I was a college kid at the University of Utah, switching majors like a boat drifting through fog. I started off in pre-med, which lasted about a year. My grade point average plummeted to 1.9. I wasn't prepared for the work, didn't really understand what it took to pursue medicine.

I switched to zoology. That didn't work either.

Finally, I settled on geography. Why? I liked maps. Remember that kid in the car on family road trips? That was about the extent of my reasoning. No grand plan, no sense of calling. Just...maps seemed interesting.

Even with my love of maps, I was, to put it plainly, lost.

The only thing I knew for certain was that I wanted to join the Air

Force, because in addition to maps, I liked airplanes. Being in the military sounded like an adventure. But beyond that vague ambition, I had no real direction, no sense of purpose driving me forward. There was no real meaning in my life.

Looking back, it's clear that I was like a ship without a compass, turning in circles, going nowhere in particular. I needed something, or Someone, to point me toward True North and offer a calling to orient my life around, but I didn't know Him yet.

The Universal Call

What I've learned since then is that we all get the call to find our way back to True North. The question is whether we recognize it and respond.

Sometimes the call comes through a person who enters our lives at exactly the right moment, a friend who asks the question we've been avoiding, a mentor who sees potential we've buried, a stranger whose story mirrors our own. Sometimes it comes through a failure that forces us to reconsider everything we thought we knew about success, identity, or purpose. The job we didn't get. The relationship that ended. The dream that died. And sometimes it comes through a quiet dissatisfaction that whispers in the margins of our busy lives: *There has to be more than this.*

Sometimes we get all three at once.

The call rarely shows up in our timeframe or in the form we expect. It doesn't wait for us to be ready. It doesn't announce itself with trumpets or burning bushes. More often, it arrives disguised as disruption, something that breaks our rhythm, interrupts our plans, or exposes the gap between the life we're living and the life we were made for.

And, unfortunately, we can ignore it. We can numb it with busyness, distract ourselves with entertainment, rationalize it away with excuses. We can tell ourselves we're fine, that everyone feels this way, that it's just a phase or stress or middle age.

But the call doesn't go away. It keeps coming back, sometimes louder, sometimes quieter, but always present, because God is always calling us back to Himself.

This is how calling begins. Not with clarity, but with movement. Not with a detailed map, but with a simple invitation: "Come. Follow. Trust me to show you the way."

It's the same invitation Jesus gave to fishermen on the shore of Galilee. They didn't know where they were going. They didn't have a five-year plan. They just heard the call, and they responded.

The first step toward True North isn't having all the answers. It's being willing to take the first step without them.

Biblical Patterns of Calling

The Bible is full of these moments of calling and redirection. God rarely provides the whole map; He usually just shows the next step. For those who trust Him, this is enough.

Abraham is one example of being called out into an unknown plan. God gave him a call: "Now the LORD said to Abram, 'Go from your country and your kindred and your father's house to the land that I will show you'" (Genesis 12:1).

Notice what God didn't say. He didn't give specific directions or better yet, provide a map of the journey. This verse doesn't even indicate a direction to start off in. There is certainly not the name of a destination. Just "Go...to the land I will show you."

Think about what Abraham left behind. His home, Ur of the Chaldeans, was one of the most advanced cities of its time. Archaeological evidence shows they had running water (not a pressurized plumbing system like today, but a brilliant system of canals), a library system, and a thriving economy. Abraham wasn't escaping poverty or persecution. He was comfortable, established, and successful.

At seventy-five years old, an age when most men, even in ancient times, had likely settled down, Abraham obeyed the voice calling him to abandon everything familiar. His country (security). His people (identity). His father's household (inheritance). All for a promise: "I will show you."

Future tense. No guarantees about when or how.

Hebrews 11:8 tells us:

> By faith Abraham obeyed when he was called to go out to
> a place that he was to receive as an inheritance. And he
> went out, not knowing where he was going.

Truly Abraham belongs in that honor roll of faith heroes. His faith prompted him to move before seeing the whole path and demonstrate His trust in the Guide rather than the plan.

The Magi who followed the star, declaring the birth of Jesus, also navigated into the unknown.

> Now after Jesus was born in Bethlehem of Judea in the days of Herod the king, behold, wise men from the east came to Jerusalem, saying, "Where is he who has been born king of the Jews? For we saw his star when it rose and have come to worship him."
>
> — Matthew 2:1-2

These men fascinate me. They weren't Jewish believers waiting for the Messiah. Most likely, they were Zoroastrian priests from Persia, astrologers, scholars of the stars. This made them complete outsiders to the covenant promises of Israel.

Yet when they saw an unusual star, something in them said: "Follow."

Consider the logistics. This wasn't a weekend roadtrip. Scholars estimate their journey took anywhere from several months to two years. They had to organize a caravan, pack provisions, and navigate hostile territory. Can you imagine the conversations they had when explaining to their families they were leaving everything to follow a star?

The star didn't even take them all the way. It led to Jerusalem, where these foreign men had to ask for directions. Imagine their confusion: "We've followed this star for months, and now we're asking around like lost desert wanderers?"

But they persisted. When the star reappeared and led them to Bethlehem, "they rejoiced exceedingly with great joy" (Matthew 2:10). Partly because their journey was over, but more so because their faith in following had been vindicated.

These pagan astrologers found the Christ child because they were willing to follow the light revealed to them, even when they didn't understand where it was leading.

The Bible's recording of Jesus calling His first disciples is another example of obedient men who answered God's call even though they didn't have many answers of where they were going.

> As Jesus was walking beside the Sea of Galilee, he saw two brothers, Simon called Peter and his brother Andrew. They were casting a net into the lake, for they were fishermen. "Come, follow me," Jesus said, "and I will send you out to fish for people." At once they left their nets and followed him.
>
> — Matthew 4:18-20 NIV

All these brothers knew when they left their boat was that Jesus asked them to "Follow me."

The Greek word for "at once" is *eutheos*: immediately, without delay. These young men had responsibilities. Peter was married, and fishing was their livelihood.

Yet something in Jesus and His simple call was enough. Maybe it was the authority in Jesus' voice. Maybe they'd heard of Him previously. Maybe their hearts were so ready for purpose that any call would have moved them.

I love that the promise Jesus did make was specifically relevant: "I will make you fishers of men." He took what Andrew and Peter knew, fishing, and promised to transform it into something more, something that would matter forever.

The Pattern

Do you see the pattern within each of these calls? In each case:

- The call came during ordinary life
- It required leaving the familiar
- The full destination wasn't revealed
- The response required trust
- God used what they already had (Abraham's leadership, the Magi's understanding of the stars, the disciples' fishing) but transformed it for His purposes

This is how God works. Angels don't arrive with detailed instructions, and God doesn't typically provide the whole map upfront. He says, "Trust Me. Follow. I'll show you as we go."

Why This Journey Matters Now

You might be thinking, "That's nice for those Bible people, but what about me? I can't just drop everything and wander off following stars."

I understand. When I read these biblical accounts as a young man, they seemed simply like ancient history, inspiring stories from a different world where people could afford to be radical. I had classes to attend (or skip). Money to earn (somehow). A career to figure out (someday).

Here's what I discovered: The call to find your way doesn't require abandoning responsibility. It's about finding the purpose behind your responsibilities and moving from drifting to directed, from existing to living with intention.

The Difference Between Existing and Living

When I was drifting through college, I went through motions without meaning. I viewed my classes as requirements to check off. Grades were just letters that determined whether I'd graduate. Even my Air Force ambition was more about escape than purpose.

I was existing, not living. Surviving, not thriving. Moving, but not going anywhere. I was drifting.

Maybe you know the feeling.

You're working a job that pays the bills but drains your soul.

You maintain relationships that exist but don't flourish.

You attend church out of habit rather than hunger for God.

You make decisions based on "what's expedient" rather than "what matters."

That kind of existence is life on autopilot. You're following the flight path everyone else seems to be on, hoping it leads somewhere good. God created you for more than autopilot existence. He designed you for purpose, meaning, direction. Your life is meant to matter, to count for something beyond yourself.

What Changes Everything

What we all have to learn is that the shift from drifting through life to living with direction happens when we realize four crucial truths:

Your life is meant to go somewhere. You're not a random collection of atoms accidentally assembled. You're a created being with a Creator who had a plan in mind when He made you. As Jeremiah said to the Israelite exiles in Jeremiah 29:11, "For I know the plans I have for you, declares the LORD, plans for welfare and not for evil, to give you a future and a hope." He may have said this to a particular people at a particular time, but the promise holds for all of His people throughout every generation. It holds for you and for me.

There's a God who wants to guide you. We aren't left alone to find our own path or create our own meaning. God has a path marked out for each person, and by faith He leads us to discover the way. Proverbs 3:5-6 promises,

> Trust in the LORD with all your heart, and do not lean on your own understanding. In all your ways acknowledge him, and he will make straight your paths.

God's wisdom is available. This was revolutionary for me. I'd been trying to navigate with my own wisdom and limited vision. But God offers His perspective and guidance. James 1:5 assures us, "If any of you lacks wisdom, let him ask God, who gives generously to all without reproach, and it will be given him."

The next step you will take is more important than knowing the whole path. You don't need God's ten-year plan. You need to know what God wants you to do today. As Psalm 119:105 says, "Your word is a lamp to my feet and a light to my path." Notice it's a lamp, not a searchlight—only suitable to show the next step, not the next mile.

The Promise of Spiritual Navigation

Here's the promise that changed my life: As sailors can search the stars for direction in navigation, we can go to God for direction in our lives. Just as certainly as a compass points north, the Holy Spirit points toward truth. Maps are reliable to show terrain, and Scripture is our resource to understand the spiritual landscape.

Think about it. For thousands of years, sailors crossed vast oceans with primitive tools:

- A sextant to measure the angle of celestial bodies
- A compass to find magnetic north
- Charts crudely drawn by those who'd sailed before
- The accumulated wisdom of experienced mariners

That these tools worked baffles me, but they did. Explorers found new continents, established trade routes, and connected the world.

If human beings can navigate physical oceans with physical tools, how much more can we navigate life with the spiritual tools God provides? He who created the stars can surely guide us by them. He who established magnetic north can point our internal compass. He who inspired Scripture can illuminate our path through it.

But—and this is crucial—first you have to answer the call to stop drifting and start navigating.

This Isn't About Perfection

Let me be clear: This isn't about becoming super-spiritual or having all the answers. I didn't suddenly transform from a drifting college student into some kind of spiritual giant. I didn't wake up one morning with perfect clarity about my calling or a direct download from heaven about my future. God didn't hand me a leather-bound life plan with my name embossed on the cover.

What happened was simpler, and more profound, than that. God revealed the path He had for me not all at once, but step by step, through ordinary circumstances and quiet realizations. He led me through these transformations:

From self-reliance to God-reliance. I stopped pretending I had it all figured out and admitted I needed help. I'd spent years trying to prove I was capable, independent, self-sufficient. But that posture was exhausting, and it was keeping me from the very guidance I needed most. Asking for help wasn't weakness. It was wisdom.

From random to purposeful. I stopped making decisions based solely on what seemed interesting, easy, or immediately gratifying, and started asking what God might actually want. Not in some mystical, hear-voices-from-the-sky way, but in a "What matters eternally? What aligns with who God made me to be? What serves others rather than just serving myself?" kind of way.

From alone to guided. I stopped trying to navigate solo and accepted that God actually wanted to direct my path. I'd been operating under the assumption that faith meant figuring things out on my own and then asking God to bless my plans. But real faith is the opposite: It's trusting God enough to follow even when the path isn't fully visible yet.

These shifts didn't happen overnight. They happened in increments, through small choices and stumbling steps. And they're still happening. I'm still learning. Still recalibrating. Still finding my way back to True North when I drift.

We've all experienced times of being lost. Maybe you've circled the same gas station three times in five minutes, staring at your GPS in frustration, realizing you have no idea which route to take. Or maybe you've stood in the parking lot of a massive shopping mall, completely disoriented, unable to remember where you parked. In those moments, there's a very specific feeling: the sudden, uncomfortable awareness that you don't know where you are, and the equally uncomfortable realization that you need to stop, reassess, and ask for help.

These moments of being physically lost are annoying, even humiliating. But they're also clarifying. Eventually, it becomes undeniable: I'm lost. I need help. I can't figure this out on my own.

Spiritual disorientation works the same way. We can ignore it for a while. We can keep circling, hoping things will suddenly make sense. But eventually, if we're honest, we have to admit: *I don't know where I'm going. I don't know what I'm doing. I need help.*

And that's not failure. That's the beginning of reorientation.

Those times of feeling lost, whether sudden or slow-building, are often God's invitation. He may have brought us to this place of dissatisfaction, confusion, or crisis not to punish us, but to call us back. To wake us up. To offer us something more than what we've been settling for.

The question is: Will we recognize the invitation? And will we respond?

Signs You're Being Called

That restlessness you feel? That sense that you're meant for something more? That's not a flaw in your character. That's the homing beacon God placed in your soul, calling you back to Him and forward to purpose. But how do we really know God's voice? What are indications that He is calling us to a particular path? Look for these signs:

First you might experience "holy dissatisfaction." That's what I call the nagging sense that there has to be more to life. The feeling that you're made for something beyond what you're currently doing. This isn't depression or ingratitude, it's your soul telling you it's time to move.

I felt it in college, a restlessness that no amount of activity could satisfy. It was different from worldly ambition. Ambition says, "I want more." Holy dissatisfaction says, "I was made for more."

Maybe you feel your talents are being wasted, your time is being spent on things that won't matter in eternity, and you're playing a role rather than living your purpose. Success as the world defines it feels surprisingly empty.

This dissatisfaction often intensifies during seasons of apparent success. You might be climbing the ladder only to realize it's leaning against the wrong wall. The promotion doesn't bring fulfillment. The achievement feels hollow. The applause echoes in an empty heart.

I remember after finally getting it together academically, sitting in what should have been a moment of triumph—good grades, promising future, everyone proud of me—and feeling completely lost. The very success that was supposed to satisfy me highlighted how far I was from where I belonged. That's holy dissatisfaction at work: God using our emptiness to create hunger for something real.

Another way God gets our attention to direct the way He has for us to go is through repeated themes. That's when the same message appears from different sources. A Bible verse that keeps coming up. A conversation that echoes something you just read. A sermon that addresses exactly what you've been thinking about. When God wants to get your attention, He's not as subtle as some might think.

In my life, the themes of "purpose" and "direction" kept surfacing. Friends would randomly share how they found their calling. Books about meaning would catch my eye. Conversations would turn to

"What are you doing with your life?" Even my geography studies about navigation seemed to mock my personal lack of direction.

When you hear the same message from multiple, unconnected sources, pay attention.

These themes often start subtly. You might notice them appearing in your devotional reading, your conversations, even your entertainment choices. What begins as coincidence reveals itself as providence. The themes grow stronger and more frequent until you can't ignore them.

Sometimes the repetition comes through people. You'll find yourself having the same conversation with different friends. Strangers will share stories that eerily mirror your own questions. Your pastor will preach about exactly what you've been wrestling with, even though you haven't told anyone about your struggle.

Sometimes God uses doors and disruptions to guide us. He may close one door to point us in a new direction. My academic failures weren't *just* failures; they were redirections. What feels like disaster might be divine course correction.

When I failed at pre-med, it felt catastrophic. When zoology didn't work out, I felt like a failure. But in hindsight, I see God closing doors that would have led to the wrong destinations. He was disrupting my plans to make room for His.

These disruptions come as unexpected obstacles that force you to reconsider the next step, opportunities that disappear just when you thought they were certain, or disruptions that shake you out of a comfortable place. Sometimes they're "failures" that free you to try something new.

These disruptions often come when we're most committed to the wrong path. The more we force a door that God wants closed, the more dramatic the disruption becomes. It's like He's saying, "If you won't listen to whispers, I'll have to speak louder."

The key is learning to see setbacks as setups. That rejection letter might be protection from a job that would have derailed your calling. That relationship that ended might have been preventing you from meeting the person God has for you. That financial struggle might be teaching you dependence before blessing you with abundance.

God also has power to speak to us from the inside through resonance. When you hear truth, something inside responds. Like a tuning fork vibrating to its frequency, your soul recognizes its calling when it hears it.

You know the feeling, when someone says something or you read something and every cell in your body says "YES!" That's resonance. That's your soul recognizing truth it was designed to receive.

It might happen when a scripture suddenly comes alive with personal meaning, when someone describes a life path that makes your heart race, when you see someone living with purpose and think, "I want that," or when a possibility you'd never considered suddenly feels like home.

These aren't random emotional responses. This is your internal navigation system responding to True North.

This resonance often surprises us. You might feel it when hearing about a mission field you'd never considered, a career you'd never explored, or a calling you'd thought was beyond your abilities. The resonance isn't based on logic or practicality; it's your spirit recognizing what it was created for.

Trust this inner knowing. God placed it within you as a compass. When your spirit resonates with truth, it's because your Creator is speaking to your created purpose.

Navigation Callout: Columbus's Miscalculation

Christopher Columbus believed the Earth was much smaller than it really is. When he set sail west from Spain, he calculated he'd reach Asia in about 3,000 miles. In reality, Asia was over 10,000 miles away. If the Americas hadn't been in the way, his crew would have perished at sea.

Sometimes God saves us through our miscalculations.

Columbus thought he was sailing to the Indies. He found the New World instead. He was wrong about almost everything: the size of Earth, the distance to Asia, what he'd find. But his wrongness led to one of history's most significant discoveries.

You might be wrong about where you think you're headed. You might miscalculate the distance, misunderstand the destination, or misread the signs. But if you're willing to sail beyond sight of shore, if you're willing to follow the call even when you're not sure where it's leading, you might discover a new world you never knew existed.

Sometimes the detour is the destination. Sometimes getting lost is how you get found.

Reflection and Application

Where are you right now?

- Are you drifting like I was in college, going through motions without meaning?
- Do you feel that holy dissatisfaction, that sense that you're made for more?
- Have you been ignoring a persistent call because you're afraid of where it might lead?
- Are you waiting for a detailed map when God is only showing you the next step?

The call doesn't usually come with clarity. It comes with an invitation: "Follow me." "Trust me." "Take the next step."

You don't need to see the whole journey. You just need to respond to the invitation.

A Prayer for the Journey

God, I'm tired of drifting. I sense You calling me to something more, even if I can't see what it is. Give me the courage to respond like Abraham, to follow like the Magi, to trust like the disciples. I don't need to see the whole path; just show me the next step. Help me move from merely existing to truly living with purpose. I'm ready to stop going in circles and start following You. Amen.

Coming Up Next...

In the next chapter, we'll unpack your spiritual navigation toolkit, the practical tools God has given to help you find your way. You don't have to navigate blind. God has provided everything you need: His presence as your North Star, His Word as your map, His Spirit as your compass, and His people as your guides.

The call has been issued. Now let's learn how to navigate.

Chapter 3

Your Spiritual Navigation Toolkit

 Your word is a lamp to my feet and a light to my path.

— Psalm 119:105

In October 1972, Uruguayan Air Force Flight 571 carried a rugby team, their friends, and family across the Andes. The plane had all the right instruments. The compass was calibrated. The altimeter functioned. The radio beacons were clear. Nothing was broken. But tragedy struck when the co-pilot mistook the readings. He thought they had already cleared the mountains, when in fact they were still in the thick of them. He trusted his assumption more than the instruments, and the aircraft slammed into the side of a ridge.

The survivors would endure seventy-two days in the brutal cold before being rescued. Their story became a tale of both horror and hope, but the deeper lesson is this: Even when the tools are right, human error in using them can lead to disaster.

That's the point. Having the right tools is only half the battle. You need to know how to use them properly.

The Cartographer's Lesson

I learned this truth repeatedly during my years making maps for the Air Force. At the Air Force mapping unit where I was stationed, we still

24

made maps by hand. It was meticulous work: line by line, contour by contour. Precision mattered, because important people were going to use those maps to get somewhere and, in the process, protect the national security of the United States. A single mistake could send someone miles off course and potentially into enemy territory.

We didn't just draw roads and rivers. We studied terrain. We interpreted data. And of course, we made sure that north was always at the top. Without north at the top and clear lines that follow standards, the map is just a picture, not a tool. Maps have legends that give instructions about how to interpret the lines and symbols on the page. This guidance is what makes a map more than simply an interesting picture.

We're all navigating something. And like any good traveler, we need the right tools. But more than that, we need to know how to use them.

What's in Your Toolkit?

Here's the good news: God hasn't left us to wander blindly. He's given us what we need to find our way.

In this chapter, we'll unpack four core tools for spiritual navigation:

- God as the North Star
- The Bible as your map
- The Holy Spirit as your compass
- Spiritual resources as your map key or legend

Once you learn how to use these tools, navigating life will become more clear.

God as the North Star: Your Fixed Reference Point

We've already established that God is unchanging, like Polaris. But how do you actually navigate by this truth in daily life?

The North Star, Polaris, isn't the brightest star in the sky. But it's the most reliable. It stays fixed over the North Pole. No matter where you are in the Northern Hemisphere, it points north. All other stars, planets, and satellites spin and drift, but the North Star holds its place.

In a chaotic world, God is your steady reference point. He doesn't shift with opinion polls. He isn't governed by your emotions. In all circumstances and stages of life, God remains the same: in joy and in grief, in youth and in old age, in certainty and in suffering.

 I the LORD do not change.

— Malachi 3:6

 Jesus Christ is the same yesterday and today and forever.

— Hebrews 13:8

In Chapter 10, I'll tell more about a specific time when I needed to rely on God's unchanging characteristics. That was my missile command crisis, when I was failing evaluation after evaluation and my career was imploding, I couldn't see any way forward. But God didn't move. I couldn't see Him through the clouds of my crisis, but He was still there, fixed and faithful.

Eventually, when the right mentors appeared and my situation turned around, I realized God had been my North Star all along. I just hadn't known to look up.

If you want to know which way to go, the first step is to locate God —not just the idea of God, but the presence of God. The best place to begin is not by looking around you, but by spending time in prayer, talking to the God who never changes.

The Bible as Your Map

I like to think of the Bible as a map. There is no other guide to spiritual terrain that is more relevant or impactful than God's Word. It's full of the stories of people just like us, who wandered, trusted, stumbled, and found their way again.

Have you ever held a paper map that shows a large area on one side? You can see major highways and the basic landmarks for navigation. Then on the other side, there's a detailed version which focuses on one or more specific locations on the big-picture map. This is what I discovered once I started digging into Scripture more deeply, especially during and after a special retreat that I will describe later. It was like turning over a map and realizing there had been more detail on the other side the whole time. Suddenly I saw my life in its pages.

Years ago, before we carried around routes to anywhere in the world on our phones, I would request special maps from AAA before going on a roadtrip. These maps were called TripTiks and showed narrow strips of the location, only highlighting your planned route. They had no real orientation, no sense of True North. That's how many people use the Bible. They just look for a verse that confirms what they already want to do.

But like any map, the Bible needs to be oriented properly. If you don't know where North is, True North, in God the Father, you'll misread it. Too many people twist Scripture to fit their path instead of turning their path to fit Scripture.

We must let the Bible reorient us, not the other way around.

The Holy Spirit as Your Compass

Sailors often faced nights when clouds covered the stars and the map was useless. On those nights, the compass became their most valuable tool. It did not calm the sea or stop the wind, but it offered one vital truth: direction.

That is what the Holy Spirit does for us. Even when we cannot see clearly, when faith feels like fog and every familiar landmark has disappeared, the Spirit keeps pointing toward True North.

 When the Spirit of truth comes, He will guide you into all the truth.

— John 16:13

The Holy Spirit does not only speak through worship services or sermons. He also works through quiet conviction, inner peace, and the unease that signals we are drifting. He guides us through Scripture, through wise counsel, through circumstances, and sometimes through interruptions that we never would have chosen.

I once learned this in the most direct and painful way imaginable.

The Fall That Reoriented Me

Years ago, I was working long hours, carrying too much pressure, and ignoring the subtle ways God was trying to slow me down. Then one afternoon, I climbed a ladder to make a quick repair on the roof of my home after a storm. I set the ladder carelessly, convinced I could handle the job quickly. In a moment, it slipped, and I fell to the ground.

I remember the shock more than the pain. My back was broken in two places, though by God's mercy, my spinal cord was unharmed. I could not move. My wife was not home, but a young woman named Brooke, who was staying with us at the time, came back unexpectedly after forgetting something. She found me, called for help, and stayed with me until the ambulance arrived. She was God's provision, already in place before the fall happened.

Recovery was slow and humbling. For months I wore a brace and could do little more than rest, pray, and think. It was a season of silence, stillness, and forced dependence. At first, I felt useless. My life had always been about movement, responsibility, and getting things done. Suddenly, I could not even dress myself or drive. Yet in that still-ness, I began to sense God's presence more clearly than I had in years.

I understand now that my fall was not punishment. It was reorientation, God showing me that I had been trying to navigate life in my own strength. He was resetting my internal compass, teaching me that control is an illusion and dependence is a form of grace.

When I eventually returned to work, nothing about my job and its challenges had changed, but I had. My confidence no longer came from my abilities but from trust in the One who holds all things together. The Holy Spirit had become my true compass, and I learned to check His direction before moving forward.

Sometimes the Spirit guides with a whisper. Sometimes He gets our attention through a storm or a fall. Either way, His purpose is the same: to bring us back into alignment with True North.

Spiritual Resources: The Map Key

Every map has a legend or key that explains what the symbols mean and how to read the terrain. Without that small box of interpretation, even the most detailed map becomes a jumble of lines and colors. The same is true of spiritual life. God has given us clear tools, but if we don't know how to use them, we can still lose our way.

After my fall and recovery, I began to see how God surrounded me with people and resources that served as that legend on the map. They helped me interpret what He was already showing me. Let's look at what I see to be the key resources for navigating the spiritual life. These include: prayer, Scripture, mentors, and integration into a community of believers, the local church. True spiritual growth occurs when these become more than background practices. Allowing them to become essential navigation aids is the beginning of deeper connection with God.

Prayer

Prayer is our direct line of communication with God. It keeps our internal compass aligned with His direction. Years ago, a friend introduced me to the ACTS pattern for prayer, and it has remained a helpful guide.

- **Adoration** focuses the heart on who God is, not on what we lack.
- **Confession** realigns our soul by naming where we have strayed and asking for forgiveness.
- **Thanksgiving** opens our eyes to the ways God is already working, even when we do not see His presence clearly.
- **Supplication** prompts us to bring our needs and the needs of others to Him with humility and trust.

Biblical Teaching

Listening to faithful preaching and participating in the regular rhythm of worship keeps us grounded when we are tempted to wander into our own interpretations. Wise counsel and hearing from others who have studied the Word and listen for God's interpretation acts like the fixed surveyor's mark on a map, keeping our orientation true. The practice of gathering regularly, hearing Scripture, confessing sin, and receiving grace through Word and sacrament form a rhythm that steadies the soul.

Spiritual Mentors

God often uses people to clarify what we cannot see ourselves. In my Air Force years, experienced officers showed me what faithful leadership under pressure looked like. Later, mentors in ministry and friends in Young Life modeled joy, service, and authenticity. Mentors are like margin notes written by someone who has walked the trail before us.

They may not accompany us for every mile, but their words can keep us from taking the wrong path. Over the years, I have come to believe the guidance from others is one of the primary ways the Holy Spirit works. He places the right person beside us at the right moment, many times before we realize how much we will need their wisdom.

Christian Community

Community keeps us from believing we must travel alone. A solitary believer may survive for a time but cannot thrive. In healthy community we find correction, encouragement, and shared strength. Community turns a private journey into a shared pilgrimage.

During my recovery from falling off of the roof and later during my battle with cancer, community became the face of God's provision. Friends prayed, delivered meals, and sat quietly when words would have fallen short. They reminded me that God never calls us to walk alone.

Study Tools

Concordances, commentaries, and study Bibles help us dig deeper into God's Word. They are like magnifying glasses for the map, helping us see details that we might otherwise miss. A concordance helps trace key themes throughout Scripture, while commentaries provide historical and cultural context that gives depth to our understanding.

When prayer, biblical teaching, mentors, community, and study are used together, they create a spiritual map key that turns confusion into clarity. The same Holy Spirit who reorients us after a fall uses these resources to keep us moving in the right direction once we rise again.

How These Tools Work Together

When I was diagnosed with pancreatic cancer, all these navigation tools became essential to helping me remain aligned with God's path.

The diagnosis had come suddenly: a mass on my pancreas, confirmed malignant after biopsy. Eleven hours of surgery. When they took out lymph nodes and found cancer cells, we knew it had spread somewhere in my system.

In that storm I relied heavily on these tools because I desperately needed God's map through the struggle. The tools listed above guided my way.

- **God remained my North Star:** When everything else felt uncertain, including health, future, and even daily strength, God's character did not change. He was still sovereign, still good, still present. Even when I didn't understand, I trusted His constancy to keep me oriented.
- **Scripture became more real:** Verses I had read many times before came alive in new ways. Romans 12:12, "Be joyful in hope, patient in affliction, faithful in prayer" (NIV), wasn't just advice; it became a daily reminder of how to live. Each phrase gave me something solid to hold when my own emotions and thoughts wavered.
- **The Holy Spirit gave me peace:** It wasn't a peace I could reason my way into. By all logic I should have been overwhelmed with fear. Yet there was a stillness, a quiet assurance that God had me in His hands. That peace didn't erase the pain, but it steadied me within it.
- **My church community surrounded us:** Friends and fellow believers stepped in with meals, prayers, visits, and countless acts of service. Their presence reminded me that my family was not walking this path alone. Our church friends carried part of the weight we couldn't carry ourselves.
- **Prayer became constant:** I leaned on the ACTS pattern of adoration, confession, thanksgiving, and supplication to keep talking with God. It gave structure when my mind felt

scattered, and the practice kept me connected when words were hard to find.

No single tool would have been enough. But together, they kept me oriented even when I couldn't see the way forward.

Navigation Callout: The Longitude Problem

For centuries, sailors could easily find their latitude, how far north or south they were. But longitude, east or west, was a nightmare. One wrong guess could mean shipwreck.

The British government offered a reward of £20,000 (millions today) to anyone who could solve The Longitude Problem. A clockmaker named John Harrison finally did. He worked tirelessly to solve the problem and developed prototype after prototype until his H4 chronometer was tested in 1761. In 1762, it was deemed to be accurate for its ability to track time and therefore longitude while at sea.

The breakthrough in keeping ships on the right course didn't come from a better map. It came from a better tool.

Many of us keep crashing into the same obstacles because we haven't updated our tools. We rely on instincts or "how we were raised" instead of digging into Scripture, listening for the Spirit, or seeking guidance.

It's not enough to know where you are. You need help knowing what time it is, and what direction to go next.

Reflection and Application

Which of these tools do you already have in your hands? Which are you missing?

- Are you reading the Bible like a living map, or just an old book?
- Are you tuning in to the Spirit, or ignoring that inner tug?
- Are you seeking guidance from wise mentors, or trying to go it alone?

You don't need to master everything overnight. Just begin. Pick up the compass. Unfold the map. Start listening with a teachable spirit.

A Prayer for Clarity

Lord, thank You for not leaving me to figure life out on my own. Thank You for Your Word, for Your Spirit, and for the people You've placed in my path. Help me use the tools You've given, not just to survive, but to walk with purpose. Reorient my map. Let me hear Your voice. Let me find You again. Amen.

Coming Up Next...

In the next chapter, we'll turn from the tools to the heart of the journey: how to locate God in your life right now, even if He feels hidden. We'll look back at our past through a new lens, learn how to trace the fingerprints of God, and discover that the journey toward North has already begun.

Part Two

Learning to Navigate

Chapter 4

Affliction and the Anchor

 Where shall I go from your Spirit? Or where shall I flee from your presence? If I ascend to heaven, you are there! If I make my bed in Sheol, you are there!

— Psalm 139:7–8

I n 1849, a slave and abolitionist named Harriet Tubman escaped from a Maryland plantation. She had no map, no compass, no previous knowledge, just the North Star and an iron will to be free.

"I had reasoned this out in my mind," she later said. "There was one of two things I had a right to: liberty or death. If I could not have one, I would have the other."

Night after night, Tubman followed the "Drinking Gourd," what enslaved people called the Big Dipper, using it to find Polaris, the North Star. That star meant north. North meant freedom. She traveled by night, hid by day, and kept that star in view whenever the clouds allowed.

Here's what makes Tubman's story even more remarkable: She didn't just find her own way to freedom. She went back to lead the way for others. Nineteen times she returned to the South, leading more than 300 slaves to freedom via the Underground Railroad. She never lost a single person.

"I never ran my train off the track," she said, "and I never lost a passenger."

How? She knew the direction to go, believed unwaveringly in her commitment to freedom, and never took her eyes off her goals.

The Star That Never Moves

When I trained young cartographers in the Air Force, the first lesson was always the same: Find the North Star.

Look for the Big Dipper, that constellation that looks like a cooking pot with a handle. Find the two stars that form the outer edge of the cup. Draw an imaginary line through them, extending it about five times the distance between those stars. There it is: Polaris, the North Star.

I continued their lesson by assuring them: "Now that you know where it is, you'll never not know."

That's the thing about finding God in your life. Once you truly see Him, not just the idea of Him, but His actual presence, you can't unsee Him. You start recognizing His hand in places you never noticed before. Even when you look back on the past, you realize He was there, even when you didn't know to look.

Like Harriet Tubman, once you've found your way to spiritual freedom, you can't help but want to lead others there too.

How to Identify God in Your Life

Finding God is like finding the North Star, you need to know where to look and what to look for.

First, understand that God isn't always the brightest or most obvious presence. Polaris isn't the brightest star in the sky. In fact, it ranks about 50th in brightness. But it's the most reliable because it never moves.

God often works the same way. Not in flashy or dramatic moments, but in the steady, unchanging presence that's always there. You can trust in His faithful presence whether you're acknowledging Him or not.

Second, at times it takes something outside of ourselves to highlight His presence in our lives. Just as I initially needed someone to show me how to trace from the Big Dipper to Polaris, many of us need an external force to point out the ways God is at work in our lives. Sometimes it's a person, sometimes a program, sometimes a moment of crisis that makes us finally look up.

Third, once you find Him, it takes practice to fight our human belief in independent self-sufficiency and use Him as our reference point. Knowing where North is doesn't help unless we orient our life by it.

My Journey to Faith: From Religion to Relationship

Some of my earliest memories of church don't come from home at all, but from long summer visits to my grandmother's place in South Carolina. Every other year or so, we'd pack up and drive down, and I'd spend a couple of weeks soaking in the warmth, which didn't just come from the weather.

At the end of her street stood a small Methodist church, and my Uncle "Tick Tock" would take me there. I called him that because, when I was little, I'd sit on his lap and listen to the railroad pocket watch he carried from his days as an engineer: tick-tock, tick-tock, steady and sure. Sometimes my aunts would join us for Sunday mornings, and occasionally we'd visit the Baptist church at the other end of the street. I can't tell you what was preached in those services, but I remember the kindness, the sense that the people there were glad to see me.

My aunts and uncles always made me feel welcomed. Every Sunday they'd lay out a big meal in the backyard and invite anyone who wanted to come. It didn't matter if you were family or a stranger passing through, there was a plate for you. Those Sundays were an early compass point for me. They instilled in me the understanding of welcoming faith that was consistently generous and reliable, ticking on, week after week.

I was baptized Presbyterian at fourteen, but at that point I was still a long way from understanding what baptism really meant. My parents weren't regular churchgoers. God was acknowledged but not pursued, like knowing the North Star exists somewhere up there but never using it to navigate.

Years later, as a young man drifting through college, I found myself drawn to the Catholic Church—mostly through a romantic relationship with my soon-to-be wife (more on that later), but also through a hunger

I couldn't quite name. I took classes, was baptized into the Catholic Church, but still didn't understand what a personal relationship with Christ meant.

I followed all of the motions laid out for me. Attending Mass. Following the forms. But I wasn't navigating my day-to-day life by the North Star, I was just aware it existed.

The real breakthrough in my relationship with God came through two unexpected channels: Young Life and Cursillo.

Young Life: When My Faith Became Real

By 1984, I was married with children and our family hit what seemed like a spiritual crisis. Our son had been attending CCD (Confraternity of Christian Doctrine—Catholic religious education for children who do not attend Catholic schools) when he had a terrible experience with a teacher. He came home and announced, "I'm done. I'm not going back."

My wife, in her wisdom, gave him a choice: "You're not giving up on your spiritual education. You can go back to CCD, or you can try Young Life and take your sister."

We barely knew what Young Life was, some kind of youth ministry that wasn't tied to any particular church. It seemed harmless enough.

Three months later, our son came back from a Young Life weekend retreat completely transformed. He'd sincerely given his life to Christ. The change in his life was undeniable. That weekend marked the beginning of his personal relationship with Jesus, but he continued to attend Mass with us until a little later in his spiritual journey.

The Catholic Connection

What surprised us was how well Young Life complemented our Catholic faith rather than contradicted it. The focus on Jesus, the emphasis on Scripture (especially the Gospels), the importance of community—these are all deeply Catholic values.

Young Life didn't teach our son to reject his Catholic heritage. Instead, he discovered what that heritage was really about: a personal relationship with Jesus Christ. When he later chose to join a non-denominational church, it wasn't out of rebellion but out of a desire to grow deeper in the faith Young Life had awakened.

Watching our son transform—he eventually joined Young Life staff and served for thirteen years—taught us something profound. Sometimes God uses unexpected channels to reach our hearts. It became clear to us that the best Catholic thing we did was let our child meet Jesus wherever He showed up, even in a non-denominational youth ministry.

Through Young Life, our whole family began to understand: God isn't a distant concept or a set of obligations. He's a present reality, as fixed and findable as the North Star. At the same time, He is near and present in our lives, getting our attention through whatever means will help us see Him clearly.

Cursillo: Going Deeper

Young Life showed me that faith could be alive and joyful and Cursillo showed me it could be deeply personal and transformational.

Cursillo is a Catholic retreat program, a weekend experience designed to help people encounter Christ in a profound way. There's one element of it I won't reveal (some surprises are worth preserving), but I can tell you this: It's built on the understanding that faith is caught more than taught.

The weekend is spent with other men (or women, since the retreats are held separately) who are seeking God. You share stories. You pray together. You worship. And somewhere in that experience, the clouds clear.

I went to Cursillo thinking I was being a good Catholic, supporting the church. I came back knowing I'd met Jesus personally, not as a distant historical figure or a theological concept, but as a living presence who knew me, loved me, and had been pursuing me for my entire life.

My experience that weekend built upon the understanding I had gained from walking with our son as he grew in his faith. It gave me a better perspective of God, the North Star, who I had known of for years, but perhaps hadn't known in a personal way until Cursillo.

Recognizing God's Eternal Presence

This fact, that God was navigating my life long before I knew to look for Him, amazes me.

As I reflect now, I can see His hand in:

- The way I ended up in the Air Force as a cartographer, perfectly matching my love of maps to an opportunity.
- The mentors who appeared at crucial moments in my career.
- The failures that redirected me toward better paths.
- Even the accidents and illnesses that slowed me down when I needed to pause.

My fall from the roof was perhaps one of the most dramatic "pauses" God allowed to come into my life.

As I shared in the previous chapter, that fall was not random. I believe it was God's intervention to reorient me. It happened at a time when my career had me feeling intimidated, insecure, and shrinking under pressure. I am thankful now that God stopped me long enough to reset my compass. What seemed like disaster became a turning point that gave me new strength, clarity, and faith.

It's not as though I had turned my back on God or made a deliberate decision to disobey Him. Simply, little choices I made veered me slightly away from my relationship with Him. Navigators understand the way even a small drift can leave you miles off course. Sometimes the only way to reset is through a sudden, jarring event, both literally in navigation and metaphorically in life. That was my fall off the roof. Painful, humbling, disruptive, but necessary. God doesn't always whisper. Sometimes He jolts us awake to bring us back to True North.

Navigation Callout: Wobbling Earth Shifts the North Star

Did you know Polaris has not always been the North Star? In fact, it won't always be the North Star. In the Middle Ages, it became the north celestial pole, but prior to that, in biblical times, the North Star was Thuban. The shift hasn't stopped. We know that 13,000 years from now, Vega will have replaced Polaris as being the star closest to Earth's rotational axis, making it the North Star.

In the 2nd Century, the Greek astronomer Hipparchus observed differences between his own calculations and the maps being used for navigational purposes. After comparing star charts over a period of time, he confirmed a shift in the night sky. Because the entire skyscape had shifted together, he correctly concluded that it is the Earth that is shifting, not the stars.

In fact, as it rotates the Earth wobbles causing an effect called axial precession. This slow shift means that every seventy-two years, the Earth shifts by about one degree. None of us will ever know the North Star to be anything other than Polaris, but I'm fascinated that this slow shift confirms that even a small change will eventually be noticeable and change the point of orientation.

Interestingly, ancient Middle Eastern peoples oriented much of their religious life around the rising of the sun, the East. Temple entrances faced east and people relied on the sun's position in the sky to understand the time of day. This orientation around the East is why our modern day word "orientation" derives from the Latin word for east, oriens. In reality, the rising of the sun shifts throughout the year, preventing it from serving as a reliable point for navigation. The very concept the word "orientation" is based on is not actually a consistent tool for finding one's way.

As technology has improved, we now all carry around reliable navigation systems in our pockets. We are not reliant on the shifting North Star or the rising sun to orient our location. But, sometimes we are prone to orient our lives around changing circumstances that may also lead to slow shifts that take us off course. We orient our lives around seemingly stable things like success, relationships, health, even religious tradition, only to discover these are not the fixed points we thought.

Only God never moves. Only God remains unchanging and constant.

You: Finding Your North Star

Where are you in your search for God, the North Star?

- Maybe you're like I was, baptized at fourteen but not understanding what that meant for my daily life.
- Or like I was before Cursillo, religious but not really knowing God personally.

- Perhaps you've never even looked for God in your journey until now.

If that's you, here are places to begin as you seek to align with God's direction for your life:

1. Admit you need direction. You can't find North if you rely on yourself to get to the destination.
2. Look for the travelers a little further ahead. Who has God placed in your life to point the way?
3. Be open to unexpected channels. God might use a youth ministry, a retreat, or something you'd never expect.
4. Practice the presence. Once you glimpse God, seek His guidance daily. We can never completely understand the depths of His wisdom.

A Prayer for Discovery

Lord, I confess that I've been navigating without You, aware of Your existence but not looking to You as my guide. Open my eyes to see You clearly. Help me recognize where You've been in my story all along. Show me the people and experiences You're using to lead me toward You. I want to know You, not just know about You. Be my North Star. Amen.

Coming Up Next...

Now that you've found the North Star, you need to learn to read the map He's given us. In the next chapter, we'll explore how the Bible serves as your spiritual terrain guide, and how my career as an Air Force cartographer taught me to read it properly.

The star shows you which way is north. The map shows you where to go.

Chapter 5

Reading Life's Map

All Scripture is breathed out by God and profitable for teaching, for reproof, for correction, and for training in righteousness.

— 2 Timothy 3:16

When I graduated from the University of Utah with a degree in geography, the Air Force gave me an assignment that actually made sense: cartography. In those days, maps were still made by hand. No computers. No satellites. Just sharp eyes, skilled hands, and an understanding of cartographic principles.

I was placed in charge of a map-making unit filled with seasoned cartographers. These men and women were more than technicians. They were artists and scientists combined, fascinated by the precision and possibilities of maps.

They taught me an enduring truth: Every line matters. Every contour represents something real. Every symbol carries meaning. And above all, orientation determines whether the map is useful.

We worked with meticulous accuracy. A contour line off by even a millimeter could mean a fifty-foot error in elevation on the ground. A misplaced road could send supply convoys into danger. A wrong symbol could mean the difference between a safe landing zone and a fatal mistake.

The principle that guided everything was simple: North goes at the top. Always.

The First Rule of Navigation

"In real maps, north is always at the top," I used to tell new cartographers. It sounds almost too simple, but without consistent orientation, a map is just a picture.

Remember those AAA TripTiks I described earlier? They were narrow strips showing only your planned route. The map was always printed so that the direction of travel pointed upward. Today's phone apps do the same thing by default. That's convenient for following a pre-planned path, but it is useless for actual navigation.

If you need to find your bearings, you cannot use a map that shifts depending on where you are going. You need true orientation. Otherwise, you cannot align the map with a compass, and you cannot compare the symbols on the page with the landmarks around you.

This principle—north at the top—seems obvious. Yet many people try to navigate life with maps that are turned sideways, upside down, or skewed. They may have the right information in front of them, but without orientation to True North, they interpret it wrongly.

They are like the co-pilot in that Uruguayan crash: equipped with tools that could have saved them, but fatally ignoring what those tools were actually saying.

From Physical Maps to Spiritual Territory

During those years of drawing elevation lines and marking terrain features, I was learning something deeper than cartography. I was learning how to read terrain, interpret symbols, and understand the relationship between a map and the reality it represents.

Yet I wasn't relating that understanding to the value in using the Bible as my spiritual map. Not yet.

Although I had been baptized twice—as a Presbyterian teenager and later as a Catholic—and I attended Mass regularly, I was like someone carrying a map but never unfolding it. I had Scripture, but didn't know how to read the terrain it described. I had religious knowl-edge, but no orientation to make sense of it.

Years later, after Young Life and Cursillo helped me find my North Star, I realized: the Bible isn't a rule book or a collection of inspirational quotes. It's a map. A spiritual terrain guide. And like any map, you need to know how to read it.

The Bible as Your Terrain Guide

Topographical maps do not just show flat outlines of geography; they reveal the shape of the land itself. With careful lines and symbols, they describe hills, valleys, rivers, cliffs, and roads. For a hiker or pilot, this information could mean the difference between life and death.

The Bible functions the same way in spiritual life. It is not merely a book of rules or abstract theology, but rather a terrain guide for real people navigating real life with all of its elevation changes, dry places, steep climbs, and breathtaking vistas.

Think about these parallels:

- **Elevation changes (spiritual highs and valleys).** On a map, contour lines tell you whether you are climbing or descending. In Scripture, we find both literal mountaintop encounters with God (Moses on Sinai, Elijah on Carmel, Jesus on the Mount of Transfiguration) and valleys of despair (David hiding in caves, Jeremiah weeping, Jesus in Gethsemane). These stories remind us that faith will carry us through both spiritual peaks and low places.
- **Water sources (spiritual refreshment).** For ancient travelers, knowing the location of streams, wells, and rivers was essential for survival. The Bible points us to living water, namely found in Jesus. In John 4, Jesus tells the Samaritan woman that whoever drinks the water He gives will never thirst. John also records Jesus' declaration that streams of living water will flow from the hearts of those who believe in Him (John 7:37-38). Water on a map means life. Water in Scripture means the Spirit's sustaining presence.
- **Difficult terrain (trials and challenges).** Maps warn you where the ground will be treacherous: steep cliffs, deserts,

swamps. Scripture also shows us the dangerous and difficult experiences we may face. There's the wilderness wanderings of Israel, the persecution of the early church, and the hardships Paul endured. By reading these accounts, we learn not to be surprised when our own road is difficult. God prepares us for trials by showing us how others endured theirs.

- **Established paths (the ways others have successfully traveled).** Maps show trails carved out by those who went ahead of us. Likewise, Hebrews 11 gives us the "hall of faith," the lives of men and women who trusted God step by step. Their examples mark the trail. The psalms, prayers, and epistles of Scripture are well-worn routes showing us how to walk in righteousness.
- **Dangerous areas (temptations and pitfalls to avoid).** Maps mark swamps, minefields, and cliffs. The Bible marks spiritual dangers just as clearly. It warns against greed, pride, idolatry, and sexual immorality. It gives stories like Samson, Saul, and Judas not merely as history but as cautionary signs: "Do not go this way."
- **Landmarks (spiritual truths that help you locate yourself).** Travelers need fixed points to confirm their position: mountains, towers, rivers. Spiritually, God gives us landmarks such as His promises, His covenant faithfulness, the cross of Christ, and the resurrection. Whenever we lose our sense of place, we return to these fixed truths to reorient our lives.

The Bible contains a variety of spiritual map features. Yet just as a hiker can hold a perfect map and still wander in circles if he does not know how to read it, so too can we have the Scriptures in our hands and remain lost if we do not know how to interpret and apply them.

Learning the Language of the Map

In cartography, every map speaks a language through its symbols, colors, and lines. These contribute to the whole message of the map and when considered all together, they provide more specific information to the map's user. When we take a look at God's Word from the perspective of its value as a guide, we want to first remember that the Bible is a picture of God's love in an overarching theme. It's beautiful because we can trace God's hand from the beginning to the end of time.

At the same time, the Bible is made up of different parts which we can apply to various situations of our life's journey. Let's take a look at several ways cartographers add additional information to maps and compare that to specific ways these physical features add insight to the real-life situations we will encounter.

Brown lines mark terrain features and contour lines show elevation. On a map, the brown lines reveal what the ground looks like, the ridges, mountains, and valleys. There are also specific contour lines that show elevation where close lines mean steep slopes and wide spacing means gentle hills. Spiritually, our faith increases and decreases as we face various circumstances. The Bible teaches how to celebrate the moments when our strength is strong, the mountaintop experiences. We read psalms of praise written by people like King David who delighted in God and the awe of the disciples who saw Jesus transfigured on the mountaintop.

For seasons of grief, when we walk through low terrain and are looking to Scripture for comfort, we weep with the prophets like Jeremiah who questioned why the way of the wicked prospers (Jeremiah 12:1) and the entire book of Lamentations. The Gospels give a picture of the ways Jesus endured being misunderstood and even crucified. His words are recorded when He told the disciples that even as He was misunderstood and persecuted, so too would His followers be (Luke 6:22-23).

Blue lines mark water. Knowing the location of rivers, streams, and lakes is a crucial aspect of understanding the message of a map. Travelers need to understand where the water is. It can mean a sought after source of refreshment and cleansing or a detour to navigate around, over, or through.

Literal and figurative water is also a frequently-used symbol in the Bible. We learn that the Holy Spirit brings rivers of living water to souls of those who believe (John 7:37-39). Jesus declares that He is Living Water (John 4) providing not simply physical refreshment, but hope and renewal. Physically, water is the key element for the sacrament of baptism. We can read about John the Baptist, who baptized Jesus, and then the directive from Jesus that we too should make disciples and baptize believers (Matthew 28:19-20).

Green areas show vegetation. Forests, parks, and grasslands are all denoted on maps through shades of green. Readers understand these to be fertile places where there is life and growth. The Bible is packed with words that not only speak life into our current circumstances, but also outline ways to grow and move forward into even fuller life. Believers are encouraged to put down roots to grow and flourish in life. Throughout the New Testament we uncover moments when Jesus and the apostles tell us where the green areas of life are and how we can move towards them in our spiritual journey. In John 15, Jesus describes Himself as the "true vine" and as we remain in Him we will produce fruit and find joy.

I love the image of the Bible as a map because it truly offers all the same guidance that an earthly map provides. Whether we are on a mountaintop, valley, looking for life, or wondering where to find growth, the Bible is the spiritual resource we need to consult. It even remains consistent with the importance of map orientation. Just as every map must align with the north, our understanding of Scripture must always be oriented to the True North of God revealed in Jesus Christ.

The Berean Method

Acts 17:11, NIV describes the Bereans:

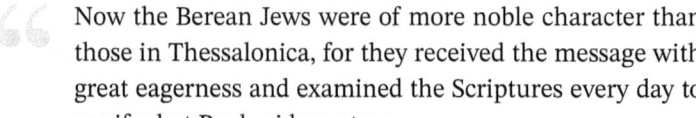

> Now the Berean Jews were of more noble character than those in Thessalonica, for they received the message with great eagerness and examined the Scriptures every day to see if what Paul said was true.

The Bereans modeled how to read a spiritual map correctly. They did not just skim the surface. They examined, compared, and scrutinized. The Greek word translated "examined" means to investigate like a lawyer preparing a case, to sift the evidence carefully.

This is exactly what skilled map readers do when trying to make a plan. We do not just assume the road is where someone says it is. We triangulate with multiple reference points. We check against established landmarks. We verify.

Spiritually, this means we test every teaching, every new idea, every stirring of conscience against the Word of God. We compare Scripture with Scripture, anchoring ourselves in what is true. This keeps us from drifting into error or being misled by those who would distort the map.

When You Need a Guide

Even while having the best maps sometimes we need a guide to show us the way. In Acts 8, Philip encounters an Ethiopian official reading Isaiah. "Do you understand what you are reading?" Philip asks (verse 30). The man answers honestly: "How can I, unless someone guides me?" (verse 31).

That humility opened the door for Philip to climb into the chariot and explain how the prophecy he had been reading pointed to Christ. God used Philip's explanation to reach the man's heart and the official was baptized that very day.

In navigation, the best military units always send out scouts. These are men who know the terrain firsthand. They can point to the shading on the map and say, "This means swamp, avoid it," or "This contour line hides a cliff face." Without their guidance, you might walk into danger unprepared.

Spiritually, we need mentors, pastors, teachers, and mature believers to help us read the map of Scripture. Sometimes they show us what we are missing. Sometimes they warn us of pitfalls we have not yet seen. Sometimes they simply confirm, "Yes, you are on the right path. Keep going."

The best map readers don't take it upon themselves and learn in isolation. In a similar way, wise spiritual seekers learn how to follow God's Word faithfully through the help of others who have walked ahead of them.

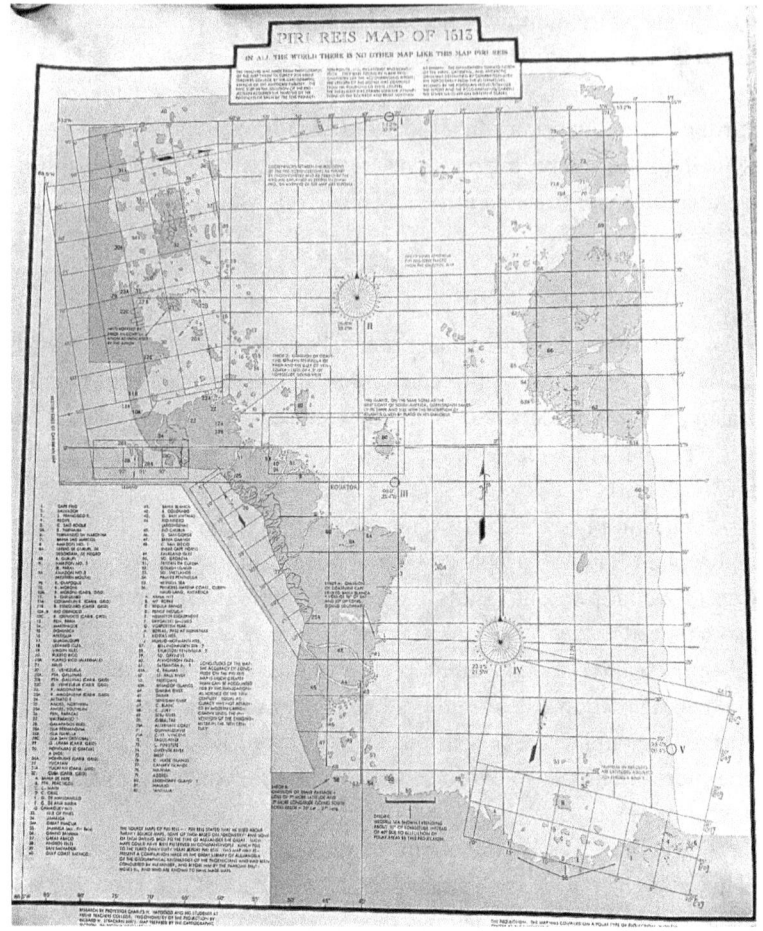

Modern rendering of the Piri Reis Map

Navigation Callout: The Piri Reis Mystery Map

In 1929, scholars discovered a fragment of a world map drawn in 1513 by Ottoman admiral Piri Reis. It showed the western coasts of Europe and Africa, the eastern coast of South America, and possibly even Antarctica's coastline.

What made it extraordinary was that Reis claimed to have compiled it from much older source maps, some dating back centuries before Columbus. His annotations listed Ptolemaic, Arabic, Portuguese, and even Columbus's maps as his sources.

The accuracy was stunning. Features like the Andes mountains and the Amazon delta appeared long before most Europeans knew of them.

The Bible is like that. Ancient words, preserved across centuries, that reveal truths we often think are new. What psychology or philosophy claims to "discover" today has often been in God's Word for thousands of years.

Orienting Your Map to True North

So how do we orient the Bible so that it functions as a true guide? How do we keep from misusing it or misreading it, and instead let it direct us faithfully?

Recognize Jesus as True North. From Genesis to Revelation, every page ultimately points to Him. Jesus Himself said to the Pharisees, "These are the very Scriptures that testify about me" (John 5:39 NIV). If we read the Old Testament without seeing the thread that leads to Christ, we miss the point. If we read the New Testament as mere moral lessons rather than revelations of His life and work, we misorient ourselves. A compass needle always swings toward north, no matter its location. In the same way, every verse of Scripture, when read rightly, draws you back to Jesus.

Read Scripture in context. One of the most common mistakes in both navigation and Bible reading is isolating a fragment and ignoring the larger picture. A hiker who looks at one square inch of a map without seeing what lies around it could walk straight to the edge of a cliff. Likewise, when we pull verses out of context to support our own agendas, we misapply them. The terrain matters. What came before? What comes after? Who was the passage written to? Without context, truth can be twisted.

Use multiple reference points. Good navigators never rely on a single landmark. They triangulate by using at least three fixed points. Spiritually, this means comparing Scripture with Scripture. Let the Psalms shed light on the Gospels. Let the words of Paul illuminate the prophets. Let the clear passages interpret the difficult ones. When you cross-check multiple truths, the map comes alive with accuracy.

Pay attention to where you are. A walking map of New York City will be quite different from a highway map of New York City. While both document the same location, they will highlight different features of the area for the various ways people will traverse the area. Spiritually, this means that it's okay to seek out the specific insights the Bible has for your current situation. A psalm of lament resonates differently when you are grieving than when you are celebrating. The story of Abraham's faith looks one way to a young believer just starting out and another way to a parent praying for a prodigal child. The circumstances you are in affects what you notice and how you apply it.

Remember the goal is not just to read the map, but to follow it. Maps are not meant to be admired. They are meant to be used. Scripture is the same. James tells us to be "doers of the word, and not hearers only" (James 1:22). If we only study God's Word without applying it, we are like travelers who trace routes with their fingers but never take a step. The real proof of reading the map correctly is found in walking the path.

When the Map Seems Wrong

Sometimes we inherit spiritual maps that are poorly oriented. They contain true features but point us in the wrong direction.

Perhaps you were taught to read the Bible as nothing more than a rule book, with God reduced to a cosmic policeman keeping score of your failures. That kind of map produces fear but not freedom.

Or maybe you were told Scripture is a collection of promises to claim, as though verses could be pulled like coupons and redeemed for blessings on demand. That map may look hopeful, but it will leave you disappointed when life's terrain does not match your expectations.

Others have been handed a weaponized Bible, a map used to attack others, justify prejudice, or enforce man-made traditions. That orientation distorts God's heart and leads people away from, not toward, His love.

I had inherited maps like that. They were heavy with fear, layered with tradition, and misaligned with the character of Christ. They left me confused and anxious rather than secure and guided.

The answer was not to throw away the map. God's Word was never the problem. The problem was orientation. Once I learned to reorient the Scriptures toward Christ as True North, what had once felt oppressive and confusing became life-giving. The same verses that had once filled me with fear began to fill me with hope, because now I was reading them in the light of the One who fulfilled them.

The Mapmaker's Wisdom

After years of making maps, I learned to recognize the difference between a decorative drawing and a functional tool. Some maps were meant to impress with ornate borders, bright colors, even mythical creatures in the margins. They were beautiful, but useless to a soldier or pilot trying to navigate real terrain. Other maps might not look as impressive, but they were precise, calibrated, and reliable. Those were the ones that could save lives.

The same is true spiritually. You can own a Bible with gold edges, full of highlighted verses and notes in the margins. You can memorize large sections and even quote them with authority. But if it is not oriented to Jesus, if you are not actually applying it to your daily steps, then it is little more than decoration.

When you finally orient the Scriptures to True North, the difference is dramatic. Suddenly the terrain makes sense. The confusing twists and turns of your life line up with the contours of God's story. You begin to see not only where you are, but also where you have been and where God is leading you.

Maps are not meant to be admired from a distance. They are meant to be trusted, unfolded, and followed. The wisdom of the true Mapmaker is that He has given us a guide we can trust completely. When we read it rightly, it does more than inform us. It moves us. It directs us. It leads us home.

Reflection and Application

Where are you in learning to read God's map?

- Have you been trying to navigate with a disoriented map?
- Are you reading fragments without seeing the whole terrain?
- Do you need guides to help you understand what you are seeing?
- Is it time to reorient your spiritual map to True North?

Start here:

1. Open the Bible with fresh eyes.
2. Look for Jesus on every page.
3. Read for navigation, not just information.
4. Find experienced guides.
5. Practice daily orientation by coming back to God's Word every day.

Remember: the map was made by the One who not only traveled the terrain but created it. Trust the Cartographer.

A Prayer for Clear Reading

Lord, I have Your map, but I need Your help to read it properly. Open my eyes to see the terrain You are describing. Help me orient everything to You as my True North. Place guides in my life who can show me what I am missing. Most of all, help me not just to read about the journey, but to walk it. Make Your Word a lamp to my feet and a light to my path. Amen.

Coming Up Next...

You have found your North Star. You are learning to read the map. But what about the times when clouds hide the stars and the map is hard to see? In the next chapter, we will explore how the Holy Spirit serves as your compass—the internal navigation system that points to True North even when you cannot see it.

Chapter 6

Using Your Compass

For we walk by faith, not by sight.

— 2 Corinthians 5:7

In 1973, I was a newly minted Minuteman missile combat crew commander at Malmstrom Air Force Base in Montana. I'd left behind my comfortable cartography career to enter the high-stakes world of nuclear deterrence. The training had been intense and took me from Vandenberg Air Force Base to squadron officer school and learning emergency war order procedures. I thought I was ready.

I wasn't.

My first evaluation in the simulator went badly. Then came the no-notice inspection in the field. I was 90 feet underground in a launch control capsule, responsible for ten Minuteman ICBMs, when the evaluators arrived. I failed. Not just a minor mistake. I failed completely. They relieved me of duty right there in the field.

The Wing Commander demoted me from crew commander to deputy. My Air Force career was circling the drain. I'd been in the service for six years, and suddenly I was failing at everything I touched. The instruments were all there: procedures, checklists, protocols. But I couldn't seem to read them right. I was navigating by panic instead of principle.

That's when something shifted. I can only describe it now as the

Holy Spirit intervening, though I didn't recognize it at the time. I wasn't walking closely with God then. We went to church, but I didn't understand what a personal relationship with Christ meant. Now I can look back and see His compass at work, pointing me toward True North even when I couldn't see the stars.

When External Navigation Fails

Every navigator knows there are times when you can't rely on what you physically see. Fog rolls in. Clouds obscure the stars. Mountains block your view of landmarks. That's when you need instruments you can trust, tools that work regardless of visibility.

In the missile field, we had a saying: "Trust your instruments, not your instincts." When you're deep underground in a launch control center, you can't see anything. There are no windows, no external reference points. Just banks of equipment and the knowledge that you're responsible for weapons that must never be used but always be ready.

My instincts during that failed evaluation had told me to panic, to second-guess, to hesitate. But instincts lie when you're under pressure. What I needed was an internal compass, something that would point true regardless of external circumstances.

The Compass Appears

Within days of my demotion, the Air Force assigned me to work with seasoned crew members. First, a veteran combat crew commander who took me under his wing. He didn't just teach me procedures. He taught me to trust the process. "Stop overthinking," he'd say. "The procedures work if you work them."

After a few weeks of intense learning I was promoted back to commander, and they paired me with an outstanding deputy, someone who knew the systems inside and out and had the patience to teach. Together, we drilled scenarios until they became second nature. More importantly, they showed me how to stay calm when evaluators arrived, how to trust my training instead of my racing heart.

Within a year, I became an instructor. A year after that, an evaluator. By 1975, I was selected for Olympic Arena, the premier missile combat competition where the best crews from across the Air Force competed. We didn't do well that first year, but in 1976, our wing swept nearly every award.

I went from the brink of career failure to representing my wing at the highest level in just three years. How? Looking back, I see it clearly: God provided human compasses when I needed them most. He used other people to guide me when I couldn't find the way myself.

Understanding Your Spiritual Compass

The Holy Spirit works like a compass: always pointing toward Himself, always near, always accurate. But like a physical compass, you have to know how to read it.

A compass points to magnetic north, which is different from true north. The difference is called declination, and means your position relative to true north varies depending on where you are. In some places, magnetic north is 20 degrees off from true north. Experienced navigators know to adjust for this.

The world offers its own version of spiritual direction. I'll call it "magnetic spirituality." It points toward something that seems like truth but isn't quite aligned with God's True North. This false guide might be success, self-fulfillment, or even religious activity without relationship with Jesus. These things aren't necessarily bad, but if you navigate by them alone, you'll end up off course.

The Holy Spirit, however, always points to true spiritual North, to God Himself, revealed in Jesus Christ. Jesus promised, "When the Spirit of truth comes, he will guide you into all the truth" (John 16:13).

Learning to Trust What You Can't See

Years later, in 1989, I faced another crisis of navigation. I'd been working at Booz Allen Hamilton for about a year when everything went sideways. A colleague in my office had been fired for security violations. Though I had nothing to do with it, the investigation cast a shadow over everyone who'd worked near him. My boss, trying to protect me, transferred me to the contracts division, a field I knew nothing about.

That's how I landed in contracts. Suddenly, I was Booz Allen's first subcontracts manager. The department was still small, maybe eight people, and I was in brand new waters. I had worked with contracts before, mostly in the Pentagon negotiating vendor agreements, but this was different. Now I was the one responsible, and it felt like being tossed into the deep end.

God gave me a good mentor, Norma Barnett, who patiently walked me through the ropes. I'll always be grateful for her guidance. But I also inherited an employee who seemed determined to make my life miserable. She was sharp, experienced, and she knew contracts inside and out. She also made it clear she wanted my job. Every decision I made, she second-guessed. Every misstep, she pounced on. I felt constantly undermined.

Between the steep learning curve, the pressure of being in a new role, and the constant harassment from someone who thought she should be in my seat, I felt small and intimidated. I carried that pressure home with me. It was as if my compass needle had started spinning, and I couldn't find my heading. The stress was crushing.

That was when I fell from my roof. My mind was constantly swirling from work pressure, and it carried over into all areas of my life. Looking back, I wonder if I had been experiencing healthier mental awareness that Saturday of my fall if I wouldn't have been so careless in putting up the ladder and it wouldn't have slid out from under me. My injuries could have been worse, but the three-month recovery was brutal.

Now, I see God at work in that terrible situation. He didn't cause my fall, but He used it. That injury took me out of a toxic work situation I couldn't escape on my own. It forced me to slow down, to stop trying to force my way through by sheer will. When I returned to work, the dynamics had shifted. I was able to have honest conversations with the difficult employee. Six months later, when the contracts division reorganized, I transferred back to my old group and spent 26 more successful years at Booz Allen.

Sometimes the Holy Spirit guides us through circumstances we'd never choose. In those moments when the compass points through the storm, not around it, He walks with us.

Biblical Foundations of Internal Navigation

Scripture is full of examples of God guiding His people when external navigation failed:

Walking by Faith: Paul wrote to the Corinthians, "We walk by faith, not by sight" (2 Corinthians 5:7). He understood that remaining close to God's path often requires trusting what we cannot see. Faith becomes our compass when sight fails.

The Pillar of Cloud and Fire: When God led Israel out of Egypt, He did not give them a map. He gave them His presence: "The LORD went before them by day in a pillar of cloud to lead them along the way, and by night in a pillar of fire to give them light" (Exodus 13:21). They could not see the destination, but they could follow the Guide.

The Still Small Voice: When Elijah fled to the mountain, devastated and afraid, God did not speak through the earthquake, wind, or fire. He spoke in "a low whisper," what the King James Version calls "a still small voice" (1 Kings 19:12). The most important navigation often comes through the quietest signals.

How the Compass Works in Real Life

In many ways the work of the Holy Spirit is countercultural. An obvious way is the manner in which He guides those who are listening. The Holy Spirit rarely shouts. Instead, He guides in the following ways:

Inner Promptings: That sense that you should call someone, take a different route, or reconsider a decision. I am grateful for the times the Holy Spirit has brought specific circumstances into my life that I know could only have come from Him. I'll go into more depth about this specific experience later, but at one point in my career when I felt stuck a friend called asking me to consider taking a new position. That's when the Holy Spirit clearly spoke to my heart telling me to "Go." The entire trajectory of my career changed from obeying that prompting.

Peace or Unrest: Colossians 3:15 says, "Let the peace of Christ rule in your hearts." The word "to rule" means "to regulate," like an umpire making the calls. When you are aligned with God's direction, there is a deep peace even in difficult circumstances. When you are off course, there is unrest even when everything looks fine externally.

Confirmation Through Others: Just as those experienced missile crewmembers mentored and became God's guidance system for me, the Holy Spirit often speaks through other believers. When I had to decide whether to leave the missile field for intelligence school or stay, I called my mentor, a colonel from my previous assignment. Without hesitation, he said, "Go to Defense Intelligence College." That confirmation aligned with what I was already sensing internally.

Circumstances Aligning: Not every open door is from God, and not every closed door is rejection. But when internal promptings, peace, wise counsel, and circumstances all point the same direction, you can trust the way the compass is pointing.

When the Compass Seems Broken

Imagine carrying a compass that appears to have lost its magnetization. The needle swings wildly or points nowhere. What then? Trusting God's direction is a reliable way to live your life, but we cannot deny that there are times when it feels impossible to sense God's direction. In those moments the needle appears to spin with too many options. Just as a physical compass can be examined to find the problem, we can examine our relationship with God to determine why we cannot sense His direction or hear the leading of the Holy Spirit.

First, check for interference. A physical compass can be thrown off by nearby metal or electronics. Spiritual compasses, our connection with God and His guidance, can be disrupted by:

- Unconfessed sin
- An unforgiving spirit
- Distractions and noise
- Exhaustion or burnout
- Fear or anxiety

Second, return to what you know. When I was failing those missile evaluations, I had stopped trusting the procedures I had learned. I was trying to navigate by feelings instead of training. Sometimes the Holy Spirit's guidance is simply, "Do what you already know is right."

Third, wait. Isaiah 40:31 promises, "They who wait for the LORD shall renew their strength." Sometimes the compass is not broken. We are simply in a magnetic anomaly zone where patience is required. God desires our growth more than our comfort. He may allow us to walk through a season when His voice feels distant.

Calibrating Your Compass

A compass needs regular calibration to remain accurate. Of course, God does not change and never drifts off balance, but in the spiritual sense it is the user who needs recalibration to connect fully with Him. Here is how to keep your connection with the Holy Spirit true:

Scripture Saturation: The Word of God is powerful and serves as the language the Holy Spirit uses when guiding His children. In order for Him to bring God's Word to mind, we need to know and memorize the Bible.

Spiritual Community: God uses other believers as His mouthpiece to challenge, encourage, and convict. Do not be afraid to seek out mature believers for spiritual wisdom along the way.

Obedience to What You Know: James 1:22 warns against being hearers only and not doers. Each time we ignore the still small voice of the Holy Spirit, it becomes harder to hear Him the next time. Each time we obey His voice, the signal becomes clearer.

Trusting the Invisible

That day I fell off my roof, I could not see how God was working. All of the results felt like disaster: compressed vertebrae, three months in a brace, career in chaos. But the Holy Spirit guided my steps even then, using what looked like catastrophe to redirect my path.

The Spirit's navigation does not always make sense at the moment. Sometimes His guidance looks like failure, like my missile field crisis. Sometimes it looks like an injury, like my fall. Sometimes He guides through simplicity, like a phone call from a friend. The key is learning to trust the compass even when you cannot see where it is pointing.

Navigation Callout: Magnetic vs. True North

Did you know magnetic north moves? In the 2000s it was shifting at a peak speed of 31 miles annually. In recent years, its movement has slowed to 22 miles per year. Ships that rely on old magnetic readings will likely find themselves dangerously off course. Sea navigation charts must be updated constantly to account for this drift.

But True North, the actual axis of Earth's rotation, never moves.

The world's wisdom is like magnetic north. It seems stable but actually shifts with cultural currents. What was considered "north" for society 50 years ago points somewhere else entirely today. If you navigate by the world's compass alone, you will drift with it.

Only God's Spirit points to True North, the unchanging nature of God Himself. While everything else shifts, He remains constant. "Jesus Christ is the same yesterday and today and forever" (Hebrews 13:8). The Holy Spirit always points to Him.

In order to remain on God's path, it is crucial that we do not rely on social consensus or even religious tradition. We thrive when we maintain a living connection to the never-changing God through His Spirit.

Reflection and Application

Where are you in learning to trust the Holy Spirit's guidance?

- Do you recognize His promptings, or do you dismiss them as coincidence?
- Are you navigating by external circumstances alone, or checking your spiritual compass?
- What might be interfering with your spiritual compass reading?
- When was the last time you followed an internal prompting from the Holy Spirit even though it did not make logical sense?

Start here:

1. Clear the interference. Deal with any known sin, unforgiveness, or distraction.
2. Practice listening. Set aside quiet time not just to talk to God but to listen.
3. Test the compass. When you sense a prompting, check it against Scripture and wise counsel.
4. Take small steps. You do not have to see the whole path, just the next step.
5. Record the results. Keep track of times you followed the Spirit's lead and write down what happened.

Remember: The compass works even when you cannot see the stars.

A Prayer for Guidance

Lord, I confess I often try to navigate by what I can see instead of trusting Your Spirit. Thank You for providing a spiritual compass that always points to You. Clear away anything that is interfering with my ability to hear You. Help me recognize Your promptings and give me courage to follow them, even when I cannot see where they lead. Teach me to walk by faith, not by sight. Be my guide when the way forward is dark. Amen.

Coming Up Next...

You have found your North Star. You are learning to read the map. You understand how the compass works. But there is more to navigation than these tools alone. In the next chapter, we will explore the "map keys," the essential resources God provides to help decode spiritual terrain: concordances and commentaries, church teaching, spiritual mentors, and prayer. Like a legend on a map, these tools help you understand what you are seeing and navigate with confidence.

Chapter 7

Map Keys and Legends

 Iron sharpens iron, and one man sharpens another.

— Proverbs 27:17

I n the spring of 1944, Allied forces prepared to invade Normandy with some of the finest maps ever made. Aerial reconnaissance captured the fields, roads, and buildings in sharp detail. Military cartographers checked and rechecked routes to the beaches. Planners felt they knew the terrain.

But when D-Day began on June 6, 1944, troops discovered something the maps had not prepared them for: the hedgerows of Normandy, called *bocage*. These were not garden hedges, but ancient earthen banks topped with dense vegetation—fifteen feet thick and nearly as high. Tanks like the Sherman could not break through, and infantry could not see over them. Each field became a fortified trap where German defenders had the advantage.

The hedgerows had appeared as thin lines on the maps, nothing more. Yet on the ground they were walls. Only through the ingenuity of soldiers like Sgt. Curtis G. Culin, who devised the "Rhino" hedgecutter, and the guidance of locals who knew the land, were the Allies able to adapt and push forward.

The lesson is clear: A map is only as useful as its key. Without interpretation, even the most detailed chart can mislead.

So it is with faith. Scripture gives us the map, but we need guides—mentors, teachers, communities, and the Holy Spirit—to explain what its lines and symbols mean.

The Power of Interpretation

During my years as an Air Force cartographer, I learned that raw data means very little without a key. We could capture the terrain in perfect detail. Every ridge, every riverbed, every structure could be measured and recorded with precision. Yet until someone interpreted what those lines and colors represented, the map was nothing more than a flat sheet of information. It looked impressive, but it could not guide anyone.

I have seen this same principle at work in spiritual life. It is possible to know Scripture well and still miss what God is saying. You can read the Bible every day, sense gentle promptings from the Spirit, and even try to keep your eyes on Christ as your North Star, yet still lose your way when you misunderstand what you are seeing.

Spiritual truth is not just about collecting information; it is about learning to read it correctly. A verse taken out of context, a feeling mistaken for divine direction, or a teaching accepted without discernment can all lead a person off course. The terrain of life is full of obstacles, like the bocage fields of Normandy that once trapped soldiers who thought they understood their maps.

The key to interpretation is humility and dependence on God. We need the Holy Spirit to reveal meaning, and we need trusted guides and community to confirm it. When Scripture is read in prayer, in fellowship, and under the Spirit's guidance, we begin to understand the words of Scripture with more depth and clarity.

Embracing Community: Our First Key

When our son returned from a Young Life retreat in 1984, transformed by his encounter with Christ, my wife and I realized that I needed help reading my own spiritual map. Tami had been reading hers faithfully since her first communion. I was attending Mass, but faith still felt like following rules and rituals without knowing the Person behind them.

Through Young Life, we joined a community that showed us how to interpret what had always been in front of us. Leaders modeled joyful Christianity. They read the Gospels as living truth, applying stories of Jesus directly to their daily lives. They showed us that following Christ was not about perfection but direction—walking together toward Him.

What struck us was not a contradiction with our Catholic heritage, but a complement to it. The focus on Jesus, Scripture, and community resonated with the deepest values of our faith and not only grew in our faith, but became deeply involved with Young Life. After over forty years of serving on Young Life committees, we have seen our children grow into adults who now carry that same sense of joy and community into their churches.

Young Life gave us our first "map legend." It made Christianity make sense in practical, relational ways.

The Multiplication of Guides

Later, Cursillo provided another essential key for our journey. Where Young Life had filled our lives with joy, laughter, and relational energy, Cursillo invited us into quiet reflection. It deepened the roots that Young Life had helped to grow. Its leaders taught us practical applications for prayer and reading Scripture. Not only did we learn about prayer but also how to enter into prayer. They taught us not only about Scripture but how to let Scripture examine our hearts.

I began to see that this is how God works. He rarely asks any of us to navigate life alone. Instead, He provides a series of guides, each with a different gift. Communities, traditions, and individuals all serve as interpretive lenses that help us see more clearly. One mentor highlights the importance of service. Another points to stillness and contemplation. One community celebrates worship and outreach. Another focuses on teaching and depth.

Each guide brings a different light to the same map. Together they help us see its full dimension. What I once thought of as conflicting perspectives I now recognize as complementary. When viewed together, they give a fuller picture of the journey toward Christ.

Through Cursillo, I also learned that depth does not compete with joy. The two belong together. Joy without reflection can become shallow, and reflection without joy can grow heavy. The balance of both is what keeps a traveler strong on the road.

God's design for guidance is relational. He sends people to walk with us, not just to give us directions. Some of the people He sends stay for a lifetime, and others appear only for a season, but all have a purpose. Every one of them helps interpret a part of the map that we could not have understood on our own.

You can be fully devoted to Christ as an individual, but something essential happens when you become rooted in a living, breathing church community. Isolation breeds confusion, while shared faith brings clarity. A vibrant community sharpens the believer, confirms the Spirit's voice, and keeps the heart aligned with the True North that is Christ.

Concordances and Commentaries: Decoding Scripture

Alongside community, God has given us tools to help us read His Word with clarity and care. A concordance is one of the simplest yet most powerful. It allows us to trace a single word or idea across the entire Bible. By following that thread from Genesis to Revelation, we can see how God weaves His truth through every page.

A commentary does something similar in a different way. It opens the window to the world behind the text. Authors explain history, culture, and language so we can understand not just what was written but why it was written. These resources act like experienced guides who can walk us through the terrain and explain what the symbols mean. They do not replace the Holy Spirit's voice, but they help us hear it more clearly.

Using these tools reminds me of studying aerial maps during my military years. The satellite images gave me information, but the key and the notes told me what I was actually looking at. Without that insight, the data meant nothing. In the same way, a concordance or commentary helps the Scriptures rise from the page and take on meaning that is both historical and personal.

These guides are not meant to do our thinking for us. They are meant to train us to think with greater depth and reverence. When used with prayer and humility, they become instruments of discovery and have power to lead us not just to knowledge but to awe.

Church and Preaching: Expert Guides

Good preaching illuminates Scripture in the same way a skilled cartographer explains terrain features. A preacher can describe the contours of a passage so that we can see the rises and valleys of its meaning.

Catholic liturgy provides structure and rhythm for my life. It taught me the importance of sacred time, repetition, and reverence. Protestant preaching added a different kind of strength. It called me to apply truth, to engage my mind and will, and to live out what I professed.

Together these influences have shaped my understanding of Scripture. The form and structure of liturgy gave me an anchor. The energy and depth of preaching gave me propulsion. Each added something to the legend of my spiritual map. The combination has kept me balanced. One reminds me to worship with awe, the other calls me to walk in obedience. Both lead toward Christ.

When we listen to faithful preaching, we allow someone gifted by God to interpret the landscape before us. They help us see the connections between passages and how they converge on the story of redemption. The church's role is to make sure the map is read correctly, and preaching is one of its clearest ways of doing so.

Spiritual Mentors: Personal Guides

Books and sermons can point us in the right direction, but nothing replaces the presence of a personal guide. Mentors are living keys. They are people who have walked through valleys, climbed mountains, and can tell you where the footing is uncertain.

My military career was seasoned with officers who taught me how to face setbacks without losing courage. They did not just lecture about leadership. They stood beside me in the hard moments and modeled it.

Spiritually, my guides have come from many places:

- A friend who introduced me to the ACTS prayer format, turning prayer from panic into relationship.
- Young Life leaders who revealed that faith could be joyful and unforced.
- Cursillo team members who showed me the power of contemplative silence.

- Believers who were honest about their scars and failures, allowing me to see that suffering can be a path to wisdom.
- Even two women I had never met before who prayed for me outside a cancer center at the exact moment I needed hope.

Each one of these guides offered a different key for reading the map of faith. Some handed me tools for prayer. Others showed me how to find peace in waiting. Still others demonstrated what courage looks like in weakness.

Mentorship is one of God's most personal ways of providing direction. A map can tell you the distance, but a guide can tell you what the climb actually feels like. They have wisdom to share from their own experience of being redeemed by grace.

When Guides Disagree

At times, the voices of our guides will not agree. One tradition will emphasize grace. Another will emphasize obedience. One mentor may tell you to wait, to be still and trust that God will act. Another will encourage you to step forward in faith and take bold initiative.

For a long time, this confused me. I wanted clarity. I wanted one clear voice to tell me what was right. Instead, I often found myself standing at a crossroads between equally sincere people who loved God but saw things differently.

Eventually, I learned that disagreement does not always mean contradiction. Sometimes it means perspective. Just as two travelers can look at the same mountain from different sides and describe different views, believers can look at the same truth from different angles.

Different keys unlock different doors. One mentor helps you understand grace when you are burdened by guilt. Another teaches you discipline when your faith has grown lazy. One community nurtures reflection and silence. Another calls you to action and service. Both are necessary at different points in the journey.

The goal is not to choose sides but to remain oriented toward True North, which is Christ Himself. When He remains the center, diverse voices can sharpen rather than divide. Even tension between perspectives can become a gift. It can stretch us beyond our narrow understanding and remind us that God's truth is always larger than our grasp of it.

I have come to see these differences as part of God's design. He uses many voices to shape us. Some comfort, some challenge, and some correct. Taken together, they help us see the full landscape of faith. The important thing is to keep the compass steady and the heart humble.

If Christ is the direction of travel, the various guides along the way will each play their part in helping us reach the same destination.

Don't Let Modern Keys Confuse

We live in a remarkable time. Never in history have believers had access to so many spiritual tools. With a few clicks, we can listen to a dozen sermons in a morning, read countless Bible translations, join online studies, and follow respected teachers from around the world. For a seeker of truth, this abundance can feel like standing in a vast library with every door unlocked.

Yet that same abundance can lead to confusion. The voices do not all say the same thing, and even when they do, the sheer volume can drown out the still, small voice of God. The problem is not the presence of resources but the loss of discernment. Too often we trade depth for variety. We scroll from one teacher to another without ever letting truth take root in our lives.

Modern tools are gifts, but they are not replacements for personal engagement. A podcast can inspire you, but it cannot know you. A Bible app can remind you to read, but it cannot correct your heart without you actually reading it. True growth still happens in the slow, embodied rhythms of real community, prayer, worship, and obedience.

The digital world offers information. The Spirit offers transformation. The first can fill your mind. The second renews your life.

Whenever I explore new resources, I return to three simple questions:

1. Does this teaching draw me closer to Jesus, or does it distract me from Him?
2. Does it align with the clear teaching of Scripture?
3. Does it increase my love for God and for people?

If the answer to any of those questions is no, I set it aside.

Technology can make learning faster, but wisdom still grows slowly. The best spiritual keys have always been the same: Scripture, prayer, community, and the guidance of the Holy Spirit. These are the instruments that never lose calibration.

So use the modern keys, but test them carefully. Keep the Bible open beside you. Stay connected to the local church that knows your name. Seek mentors who can look you in the eye. The internet may offer millions of voices, but only a few will truly help you find your way home.

Navigation Callout: Here Be Dragons

Medieval mapmakers sometimes wrote the words "Here be dragons" on the edges of their charts. It was their way of admitting mystery. They had mapped what they could, but beyond that lay the unknown, and perhaps danger.

Faith has its own uncharted places. Some paths lead to truth, while others turn quietly toward distortion. False teachings, shallow shortcuts, and manipulative leaders can all appear inviting at first. The symbols look familiar, but the direction is wrong.

That is why good map keys not only guide; they also warn. The Holy Spirit gives discernment to notice when something feels off, when a teaching pulls us away from the character of Christ or the witness of Scripture.

Following Jesus is not about avoiding every risk, but about knowing the difference between exploration and drift. The safest place to be is not where everything is familiar, but where your compass is still fixed on True North.

Maximizing the Keys

Keys are only useful if we actually commit to using them. Over the years, I've found five practices that make all the difference:

- **Approach with humility.**

A person who believes they already know everything on the map has little use for a key. Spiritually, pride is the same. If I come to Scripture or to a mentor convinced I already have the answers, I won't learn. But when I approach with humility—acknowledging that I might have blind spots and need guidance—suddenly the symbols make sense. God resists the proud but gives grace to the humble, and humility is the first step to understanding.

- **Test everything.**

Paul's words in 1 Thessalonians 5:21 are short but life-changing: "Test everything; hold fast what is good." Not every key you are handed is reliable. Some guides distort the map for their own purposes. Some commentaries are biased or shallow. Some communities mix tradition with truth in confusing ways. The safeguard is to test everything against Scripture itself, to check if the interpretation aligns with God's revealed truth. The Bible is the benchmark by which all other keys are measured.

- **Look for patterns.**

When I was a cartographer, one single data point didn't convince me of a mountain's location. I looked for multiple lines of evidence. Spiritually, God often confirms His direction by repetition—through Scripture, sermons, conversations, or circumstances. When three or four keys all point to the same landmark, I pay attention. The pattern is usually God's way of underlining His message.

- **Apply what you learn.**

James warns us not to be hearers only, deceiving ourselves. If I spend my time studying the legend but never step into the terrain, what good is it? A map key has value only when it enhances how I travel. Every time I learn something new about prayer, forgiveness, or generosity, I need to put it into practice. Otherwise, the lesson remains theory instead of transformation.

- **Pass it on.**

Teaching is one of the best ways to internalize navigation skills. As I've mentored younger believers, I've realized that their questions sharpen my own understanding. When you help someone else read the map, your own reading improves. That's why Proverbs 27:17 says, "Iron sharpens iron." We become better navigators when we guide others.

Personal Libraries and Arsenals

Over the years, I've collected keys and tools that help me navigate. I've mentioned these valuable keys previously, but because these are dear to me, I'd like to share about my favorites.

- **A well-marked Bible.**

My Bible is full of underlines, notes in the margins, and dates that remind me where God met me. Those markings turn it from a printed book into a personal history with God.

- **Trusted commentaries.**

Not every commentary is equal, but the ones that have proven faithful over time are like trusted guides I can turn to when I face a confusing passage. They provide cultural background, language insights, and theological depth I would miss on my own.

- **Notebooks and journals.**

I keep sermon notes, personal reflections, and prayers in notebooks. Looking back through them is like retracing my own journey. They remind me of lessons I've learned, prayers God has answered, and ways He's shaped me through the years.

- **Mentors and friends.**

I have phone numbers and emails of people I know I can call when I'm confused or discouraged. Sometimes one short conversation with a long-time believer is worth more than a library of books.

- **Spiritual communities.**

A local church, small groups, and ministries like Young Life and Cursillo have given me people who know my story, pray for me, and hold me accountable. They are part of my navigation arsenal—reminders that God designed us to walk together.

I don't mention these simply as trophies to be admired on my shelf. In fact, these are tools that I sometimes refer to on a daily basis, the way a pilot checks instruments before every takeoff or a navigator keeps charts at the ready.

Remember Your Compass

In the previous chapter we talked about the Holy Spirit as our compass. He uses these tools to speak truth into our lives. However even though all of these tools—commentaries, concordances, study guides, sermons, small groups—are valuable and useful, we must not forget to consult directly with the Holy Spirit, our compass who always points to True North. He always aligns with God's will and always whispers the way forward even when the terrain feels unfamiliar.

It is possible to bury yourself in study tools and miss the voice of the Spirit. A soldier with every map in the world but no working compass will still lose his way. Likewise, a believer with shelves of resources but no living connection with God will struggle to find direction.

The Spirit's role is not to replace the map keys, but to make them come alive. When you read Scripture, the Spirit illuminates the words so they strike the heart. When you hear a sermon, the Spirit applies it personally to your situation. When you sit with a mentor, the Spirit highlights what is meant for you in this season.

The Spirit is not an optional add-on for navigation—He is essential. Without Him, even the clearest instructions turn into confusion. With Him, even limited resources become enough. Remember your compass. Rely on His quiet direction, and allow every other key to be secondary to His voice.

Building Your Navigation Library

God has not left you without resources. He has already placed map keys in your life. The question is whether you recognize them and whether you are willing to use them.

- **What map keys has God already provided for you?**

Pause and take inventory. Maybe you have a Bible study group that has walked with you for years. Maybe you have an older believer who calls you every few months to check in. Perhaps your childhood pastor planted truths that still guide you today. Write these down. Identifying what you already have will help you appreciate the resources within reach.

- **Who are your mentors?**

Mentors are those who have walked further on the journey and are willing to share lessons they have learned along the way. They may not have every answer, but they are living proof that the terrain can be crossed and can bring encouragement as you navigate through your own journey. Do you have someone you can call when you are facing a difficult decision? If not, begin praying for a person like that and look for someone a few steps ahead of you in faith.

- **Which communities hold you accountable?**

Walking alone increases your risk of getting lost. A local church, a Bible study, or even a few trusted friends can act as fellow travelers who keep you on course. If you have drifted from Christian community, now is the time to re-engage. Accountability is not about judgment—it is about safety on the journey.

- **What study tools do you rely on?**

Do you have a good study Bible, a concordance, or a devotional guide that helps you dig deeper? Do you use a prayer journal or Bible app to stay consistent? Tools do not replace the Spirit, but they sharpen your understanding. Consider what you already own and what you might need to add.

- **Where are you missing support?**

Sometimes the missing key is obvious. You may have tools but no mentors. Or you may have community but no personal study habits. Where are the gaps in your library? Identifying them is the first step toward filling them.

Reflection and Application

Do not wait until you are in crisis to gather your resources. Build your navigation library now:

- **Invest in tools.** Get a reliable study Bible, a concordance, and one or two commentaries you trust.
- **Connect with community.** Commit to a church, a small group, or a ministry where people know your name and your story.
- **Identify mentors.** Seek out men and women of faith who have navigated the terrain ahead of you.
- **Develop prayer rhythms.** Prayer is one of the most powerful keys. Structure it if you need to. Try ACTS, journaling, or daily set times.
- **Stay teachable.** Even when you think you know the way, remain open. God often uses surprising guides to show us the next step.

Remember, your navigation library is not a museum collection. It is an active, working arsenal designed to help you walk faithfully.

A Prayer for Guidance and Guides

Lord, thank You for not leaving me to navigate alone. Thank You for the guides You have provided—in Your Word, Your Spirit, and Your people. Give me humility to learn, wisdom to discern, and grace to guide others.

Keep my compass steady on You, my True North, and help me use every key You provide to stay on Your path. Amen.

Coming Up Next...

You've aligned with the North Star, learned to read the map, to trust the compass, and to use the keys. But what happens when you actually start navigating life's terrain? In the next section, we'll explore how these tools work in real time—through relationships, careers, failures, and trials.

Part Three

Navigating Life's Terrain

Chapter 8

Finding North in Relationships

 Two are better than one, because they have a good reward for their toil. For if they fall, one will lift up his fellow.

— Ecclesiastes 4:9-10

H ere's the story I promised earlier to share. It happened in April, 1963, when I was eighteen years old and completely lost. Not physically lost; I knew exactly where I was: the University of Utah, struggling through pre-med courses with a dismal 1.9 GPA. But spiritually, emotionally, and directionally lost. My only clear goal was joining the Air Force because I liked airplanes. Beyond that vague ambition, I was drifting.

Then I met Tami.

Even though she was a year younger than me, she had something I did not: direction. Not career direction necessarily, but life direction. She knew who she was, what she believed, and where her worth came from. From the beginning of our relationship, she made one thing crystal clear. She was a faithful Catholic and would be attending church with or without me.

I had been baptized Presbyterian at fourteen but rarely attended church. Religion was something acknowledged in my family but not pursued, like knowing the North Star exists but never using it to navigate. It fascinated me that this young woman actually oriented her life by her faith. She was not preachy about it. She simply lived out her convictions naturally and confidently.

As I got to know Tami, I began to feel something change inside of me. For the first time in my life, I had meaning beyond vague ambitions. I wanted to be worthy of this girl who knew where she was going.

When Another Person Becomes Your Map

Tami's compass had been set long before we met. I'll tell you what she would say herself. Her faith took root as a little girl, the year of her First Communion in the Catholic Church in Park City, Utah. Even though she was just eight years old, it was more than a ceremony. That day she realized, in the way a child can somehow know without doubt, that God was always with her. That awareness gave her a sense of security that has guided the rest of her life.

That day of her First Communion, Tami received a holy card and a small missal, a Mass prayer book, as gifts. She keeps them to this day as tangible reminders of the moment she understood she would walk with the Lord for life.

Her parents did not attend Mass regularly, so her commitment was not about family pressure. She decided on her own to stay close to God and she followed through with steady consistency. When others slept in, Tami showed up for Mass. She prayed daily. Her faith was something she lived, not just believed.

When we began courting, it became clear that her faith was the foundation for her life. She did not waver, compromise, or apologize for putting God first. I respected that deeply. Watching her live that way, steady, purposeful, and anchored, stirred something in me. I began to see that if we were going to share a life, I wanted to share that same anchor.

Over time, I realized Tami's faith was not just her foundation. It was becoming part of mine. From her I gained a clearer understanding of how to receive salvation in Christ. With that knowledge, I gained confidence that life could have meaning and direction. Her compass was set on True North, and being with her helped me set mine there too.

Without telling her, I enrolled in Catholic classes at the Newman

Center at the University of Utah. I wanted to understand what made her faith so central to every part of her life and to share that solid ground she stood on.

The classes were very basic at first, simple catechism lessons that introduced me to the sacraments, the Mass, and the Catholic faith in general. But woven through those lessons I came to understand something deeper: why Jesus Christ should be the center of your life. I was introduced to the belief of unbroken succession of popes from Peter onward and the claim that the Catholic Church is the one Christ Himself began.

I came into those classes with curiosity but also with an ache for something more solid in my life. I believed in God, but I did not understand until then the ways God could be personally involved in each person's life, not just as an idea but as a foundation. The more I learned, the more I saw that faith was the kind of rock you could build your whole life on, a solid faith that could save your life and guide you to follow God in every season.

I kept going to church with Tami while I was in those classes, deepening my understanding of Catholicism without her even knowing. Somewhere along the way, I came to be convinced that the Catholic Church was, in fact, the Church Christ started through Peter as the first pope. That conviction became the reason I decided to enter into full communion with the Church.

When I finally told Tami that I had been attending catechism, she was shocked. She had no idea I had been taking classes, and no inkling I was preparing to become Catholic. But the surprise was a joyful one.

My Catholic baptism ceremony itself was simple. It took place in the office of the priest who was going to marry us, with just Tami and my mother joining me. At the baptismal font in his office, the priest poured the water, spoke the words, and I was received into the Catholic Church. The moment was not grand or ceremonial, but it was real, and it marked a turning point in my life.

The Mystery of Two Becoming One

We dated for about a year and four months, from April 1963 until we married in July 1964. During that time, we talked about marriage, but what strikes me now is that we never had any anxiety about it. We never questioned whether we should get married but carried an unspoken certainty that we were meant to be together, remarkable for two teenagers with no money and few prospects. We were married at the Cathedral of the Madeline in Salt Lake City, a grand church that is a wonderful landmark in the area and a place where we have visited often through the years.

After Tami and I married, everything changed. I went from drifting to driven. I worked three jobs while going to school. When our daughter was born about a year and a half after our wedding, the purpose intensified even more.

Scripture says something remarkable about marriage: "Therefore a man shall leave his father and his mother and hold fast to his wife, and they shall become one flesh" (Genesis 2:24). When I was eighteen and falling in love with Tami, I thought I understood what that meant. After sixty-one years of marriage, I am only beginning to grasp the depth of this mystery.

Saint Paul calls marriage a "profound mystery" and says it points to something even bigger: Christ's relationship with the Church (Ephesians 5:32). The union between a husband and wife is meant to be a living picture of how Christ loves His people.

Over decades of marriage, I have learned something important. This "becoming one" is not just romantic poetry. It is navigational truth. When God joins two people in marriage, He creates a new navigation system with two compasses learning to point in the same direction and two maps overlaying to show a fuller picture of the terrain.

In the Trinity we see perfect unity: Father, Son, and Holy Spirit, distinct persons yet one God. Marriage reflects this in a human way. Tami and I remain distinct individuals with our own personalities, gifts, and even some different opinions. But over the decades we have developed a unity of direction that has helped us navigate many storms.

Early in our marriage, I may have thought "becoming one" meant Tami would start thinking like me or I would start thinking like her. But that is not what happened. It has been more like two instruments in an orchestra learning to play in harmony. The violin does not become a cello, but together they create something neither could produce alone.

This spiritual mathematics, where one plus one equals one, has brought practical benefits as Tami and I have navigated life together. When I was drifting in college, Tami's steady faith became a fixed point

I could orient by. Not because she replaced God as my North Star, but because she was already oriented toward Him. Like a navigator who checks a compass against a partner's to ensure accuracy, her unwavering direction helped me find mine.

The Catholic Church teaches that marriage is a sacrament, a visible sign of invisible grace. I have lived that truth. Through Tami, God's grace became visible to me in ways I could not see on my own. When she looked at me, she saw not just the failing pre-med student with no direction, but the man God was calling me to become. Her vision became prophetic. I started becoming what she already saw.

This is part of the mystery. In marriage, we become God's navigation aids to each other. Not replacing His role, but embodying His love in tangible ways. When I could not hear God's voice clearly, I could hear it through Tami's encouragement. When I could not see the path ahead, I could see it in her confidence that God had a plan for us.

Here is the deeper mystery. This unity is not automatic. It is forged through shared navigation of life's terrain. Every challenge we have faced together, from those early days of three jobs and night school to raising children to facing cancer now, has deepened our unity. We have learned to read the same map, follow the same Star, and trust the same compass.

Tami is a breast-cancer survivor, a confident cancer warrior. She first found out about her cancer in 2011 and told herself and me that she would not let fear rule her life. At that time she had a lumpectomy and radiation. Six years later the cancer reappeared in her left lung. Again, surgery was the answer, and she is now cancer-free again. She takes one pill a day to keep the cancer away. Her attitude about her cancer has been an inspiration to me, and I have felt the same confidence through my cancer journey. She loves the Lord and has relied on Him through these years. She is my rock, we are one, and her love and encouragement have given me strength, courage, and confidence at this time in my life. Thank you, sweetheart. I love you so much.

Jesus prayed for His followers "that they may all be one, just as you, Father, are in me, and I in you" (John 17:21). This kind of unity, whether in marriage or the broader church, becomes a navigation tool for a lost world. When people see two becoming one while remaining fully themselves, they witness something supernatural. They see stability and direction that do not exist in relationships built on shifting sand.

The world offers its version of relationships, temporary alliances based on mutual benefit, feelings that come and go, and commitments that last only as long as they are convenient. But Christian marriage is meant to be different. It is a fixed point in a shifting world, a steady compass when everything else spins wildly.

I did not understand any of this theology when I was eighteen. I just knew that this seventeen-year-old girl had something I desperately needed—not just love, but direction. Through her, God was throwing me a navigational lifeline. By joining my life to hers, I did not just gain a wife. I entered into a mystery that would teach me about God Himself, about sacrificial love, about finding my true self by losing it in service to another.

That is the profound mystery Paul talks about, marriage as a navigation tool that points beyond itself to the ultimate unity between Christ and His Church. Every time Tami and I take steps in one direction together, check our bearings against each other, and help each other stay oriented to True North, we are living out a picture of the Gospel.

Family as Both Destination and Journey

As I mentioned earlier, our son's transformation through Young Life became pivotal for our entire family. It started with what looked like a setback, that negative experience with a teacher at CCD classes at our parish when he told us he was not going back. Tami, in her wisdom, did not let his participation in spiritual growth opportunities slide. That is when he chose to go to Young Life with his sister.

I've already shared how three months later he went to a Young Life retreat and came home completely changed. That was when he surrendered his life to Christ. I remember seeing a visible physical change in his eyes and even in his voice. From that point on, his faith was his own, and it reshaped how we functioned as a family.

That change in our son's life brought a new depth to our marriage. Tami and I had always shared faith as a foundation, but now we were watching it take root in our children. It gave us a shared mission to nurture what God had started in them. Our family conversations began to center more on spiritual growth, prayer, and serving together.

Our daughter's journey ran alongside her brother's. She had been part of Young Life as well. While her path unfolded differently, she also grew in her walk with the Lord. Over the years, she and her husband Tom have built their own rhythm of worship and service and are raising their children in the faith.

This is what I call the navigation network. Faith did not only shape Tami and me. It flowed through our children into our grandchildren. Now, when we gather as a family, we are not just sharing meals and memories. We are sharing life that orients around the same True North. Watching our kids guide their own families in the faith is one of the greatest confirmations that God has been directing our course over these many years.

Relationships as Navigation Tools

Throughout my career, God consistently used relationships to redirect my path. Some were brief encounters that arrived at exactly the right time. Others were friendships that lasted decades. God used one such connection In 1998 to change my career through a phone call. I had been at Booz Allen Hamilton for ten years, working in one of the Northern Virginia offices. I was contributing, but not moving forward. It felt like treading water, competent but stuck.

Then, unexpectedly, I received a call from a colleague at another Booz Allen location, someone I had worked with on a difficult government project years before. "Tom," he said, "we need someone down here to support a tough client at the Defense Advanced Research Projects Agency. You have the background, the clearances, and the experience. You are the right fit."

He knew my work and my temperament, steady under pressure and comfortable in technical discussions. That trust did not happen overnight; but had been built through small projects, late-night problem solving, and following through on my word.

That one phone call pulled me out of my rut. It opened doors to new challenges, bigger responsibilities, and relationships that would continue shaping my career.

Not every relationship is used in making life-changing opportunities. Some crucial relationships grow quietly and keep showing up at turning points. That is how it was with Tom and Joan Neary. We first met at March Air Force Base in 1969 where Tom and I served together in the same cartography unit. Later, when I transferred to Malmstrom Air Force Base, the Nearys were already there, and our friendship picked up right where it left off.

At Malmstrom, our families served together as lay Eucharistic ministers and helped lead noontime prayer gatherings. We celebrated Christmas Eve Mass side by side, shared dinners and stories, and built the kind of trust that runs deeper than shared assignments.

We crossed paths again in Washington, D.C., during later postings. Each time, the Nearys' faith and steady commitment helped me keep my compass set on True North. Like that colleague from Booz Allen, they were part of the network of relationships God used to nudge me forward whenever I might have stayed still.

The Power of Mentorship in Crisis

Remember what I shared from the experience of failing the missile evaluation? During that season I was failing evaluation after evaluation. To guide me through that, God did not send better manuals or brand-new procedures. He sent people.

I was under intense pressure. In missile operations, precision is everything. There is no room for half-steps or "close enough." The evaluations were relentless, and each time I thought I had made progress, I stumbled again. I knew my career was on the line

That is when the mentors appeared. These were experienced missileers who had been in my shoes before. Some were assigned to work alongside me, and others simply made time to check in after hours. They did not sugarcoat my weaknesses, but they also did not let me drown in them.

One officer in particular, a calm and deliberate trainer, broke down complex procedures into manageable steps. "Let's get the fundamentals perfect," he told me, "and the rest will fall into place." Another pulled me aside after a long day and said, "You have the judgment and the discipline for this. You just need to trust your training and stop over-thinking every move."

We went over scenarios again and again, running through checklists until the sequence felt as natural as breathing. Sometimes the break-through came in the middle of repetition, when I realized I was finally moving through the steps without the weight of panic pressing down on me.

These relationships did not end when the work training passed. Many of those mentors became long-term friends and colleagues I could call for advice years later. I can see now that the technical skills they gave me were important, but the confidence and resilience they modeled were even more valuable.

God knew I did not just need better information. I needed guides. In His timing, He placed the right people in the right places to walk me out of that crisis and onto stable ground.

Biblical Patterns of Relational Navigation

Scripture is full of examples where God uses relationships as His primary navigation system for guiding His people. These are applicable blueprints for how God has designed humanity to find our way together.

Ruth and Naomi: Following Someone Else's Map

When Ruth's husband died, she stood at the ultimate crossroads with Naomi, her mother-in-law who was returning to her home, a land Ruth had never been before. Ruth chose between staying in Moab, her homeland with her gods, her family, and everything familiar or move with Naomi to a foreign land where she would be an outsider. Logic said go home. Cultural expectations said go home. Even Naomi said go home.

But Ruth made the choice to go with Naomi: "Where you go I will go, and where you stay I will stay. Your people will be my people and your God my God" (Ruth 1:16 NIV). Ruth didn't just choose a relationship; she chose to follow a new map into a foreign land.

Ruth trusted Naomi to lead her to a destination unknown to her. She did not know that she would end up in the genealogy of the Messiah. She simply knew that Naomi, even in her bitterness and grief, was oriented toward the true God. This was her most important life navigational decision.

Naomi became Ruth's guide to a new way of life. She taught her the Jewish customs, introduced her to the community, and guided her to the field of Boaz. "My daughter, I must find a home for you, where you will be well provided for" (Ruth 3:1 NIV). Naomi knew the terrain, both cultural and spiritual, and helped Ruth navigate it.

This is relational navigation at its purest: one person who knows the way helping another find their path. Ruth's story shows us that sometimes God's direction comes not through a voice from heaven but through the wisdom of someone who has walked the road before us.

Jonathan and David: Holding Someone's True North When They Cannot

David's relationship with Jonathan might be the Bible's clearest example of how God uses friendship as a navigation tool. When they first met, David had just killed Goliath and been brought before King Saul. Jonathan, the crown prince, should have seen David as a threat. Instead, "the soul of Jonathan was knit to the soul of David, and Jonathan loved him as his own soul" (1 Samuel 18:1).

Jonathan recognized God's calling on David before David fully understood it himself. While David was running for his life, hiding in caves, and wondering if Samuel had been wrong to anoint him, Jonathan found him and "strengthened his hand in God" (1 Samuel 23:16).

Notice that phrase. Jonathan did not just encourage David emotionally. He strengthened David's hand in God. He helped David maintain his spiritual orientation when circumstances screamed that God had abandoned him. Jonathan said, "Do not fear, for the hand of Saul my father shall not find you. You shall be king over Israel" (1 Samuel 23:17).

Jonathan held onto David's calling even when all circumstances appeared to be against it. He stood strong, helping him navigate the difficult circumstances. Jonathan's friendship helped guide David's external compass when David's internal compass spun wildly. He reminded David of God's path when all David could see were the cave walls.

Even more remarkably, Jonathan helped David navigate while knowing it would cost him his own throne. True relational navigation sometimes means helping someone reach a destination you will not share. Jonathan's selfless friendship kept David oriented toward his God-given destiny during the darkest years of running and hiding.

When Jonathan died, David lamented, "Your love to me was extraordinary, surpassing the love of women" (2 Samuel 1:26). This was the deep gratitude of someone whose friend had been their navigation system through the wilderness years.

The Body of Christ: Navigation Through Collective Wisdom

Paul's image of the church as a body can also be applied to navigational reality. "The eye cannot say to the hand, 'I have no need of you,' nor again the head to the feet, 'I have no need of you'" (1 Corinthians 12:21). Each part provides something essential for functioning as representatives of Jesus in this shared journey.

The eye sees obstacles ahead. The ear hears warnings. The hands take God's provision and service to others. The feet carry us forward to spread the Good News along the path. Try navigating with any one part missing, and you quickly discover how much you need the whole body.

The early church met together, sold property, and shared all possessions in common (Acts 2:44-45). As the believers lived in community and grew in their faith together, they came to understand their different strengths and abilities to contribute. There were leaders such as the apostles who represent the head and the mouth as they spoke clearly and passionately about the Gospel of Jesus, casting vision and guidance on where to go. There were also those who served the needs of others, distributed possessions, and prepared food. These represent the body's hands and feet to go and serve. The collective wisdom of the body provided direction for the birth of the early Christian Church.

This pattern of the church as the Body of Christ has continued throughout time as Christianity has spread across space and time. Even today churches around the world support one another through practical and spiritual support. We continue to guide each other in moving further along our journey to deeper relationship with Jesus.

The body of Christ provides multiple perspectives, collective experience, accountability, encouragement, and practical support. God created us to need each other for guidance. The person who insists on finding their way alone is like an eye trying to walk without feet or feet trying to navigate without eyes. It is not just inefficient; it is contrary to how we are made.

In my own life, I have seen this repeatedly. When I was failing in the missile field, God sent experienced officers. When our family needed spiritual renewal, God provided Young Life leaders. When I faced career decisions, God supplied mentors with wisdom. The body of Christ has been my navigation system as much as any map or compass.

The Danger of Navigating Alone

Ecclesiastes warns, "Woe to him who is alone when he falls and has not another to lift him up" (Ecclesiastes 4:10). In navigation terms, a solo traveler who gets disoriented has no one to check their bearings against. They can wander in circles, convinced they are making progress.

The times in life when I have drifted furthest from God's path were seasons of isolation, either physical or emotional. When I was struggling in those early missile field days, part of my problem was trying to figure it out alone. Breakthrough came when God provided mentors and partners.

Using Community as Navigation Aids

Over our forty years of involvement with Young Life, Tami and I have discovered the power of spiritual community as a navigation tool. The adult committees we have served on are not just about raising funds or planning events. They are groups of believers who have become mutual navigation support. When one family faces a crisis, others who have walked that path share their maps. When someone's compass seems broken, the community helps them recalibrate.

The Church works, or should work, the same way: not just as a weekly gathering, but as a navigation network. Older couples who've weathered decades of marriage guide newlyweds. Parents who've raised faithful children encourage those in the exhausting toddler years. Those who've faced cancer, job loss, or grief walk alongside others entering those same valleys.

As part of this calling, Tami and I served as Eucharistic Ministers at the base chapel and taught CCD in our home while stationed at Malmstrom AFB in Montana, another example of how God has led us in serving Him.

The Ultimate Relationship Navigator

Human relationships, as vital as they are for navigation, can also lead us astray if they become our ultimate guide. I have watched people follow charismatic leaders off spiritual cliffs. I have seen marriages where one spouse's lack of faith slowly eroded the other's. Relationships are meant to point us toward God, not replace Him.

Jesus modeled this perfectly. He had deep friendships, worked closely with the twelve disciples, and shared special intimacy with Peter, James, and John. Yet He regularly withdrew to pray alone, keeping His Father as His True North. His human relationships supported His mission but did not define it.

Navigation Callout: Lewis and Clark's Sacagawea

When Meriwether Lewis and William Clark set out to explore the Louisiana Purchase, they had the best maps available, skilled frontiersmen, and government backing. But their expedition might have failed without a teenage Shoshone woman named Sacagawea.

Sacagawea did not just translate languages, though that was vital. She joined the expedition with her husband and newborn son and her very presence signaled peaceful intentions to tribes they encountered. War parties did not travel with women and babies. She knew which plants were edible, how to find roots in winter, and where to look for mountain passes. When their boats capsized, she saved crucial journals and supplies.

Most importantly, when they reached Shoshone territory and desperately needed horses to cross the mountains, the chief turned out to be Sacagawea's brother. The relationship she brought transformed potential enemies into allies.

Sometimes God provides the perfect traveling companion for our journey, someone whose presence, knowledge, and connections guide us in ways we never expected. They do not replace our need for God as our North Star or His Word as our map, but they help us read the terrain, avoid dangers, and find resources we did not know existed.

Reflection and Application

Looking at your own life:

- Who has God used to redirect your path?
- What relationships have helped you find your way when you were lost?
- Are you trying to navigate alone, or do you have traveling companions?
- How might God be calling you to be a guide for someone else?

Consider:

- Your spouse or closest friends. Are these relationships pointing you toward God or away from Him?
- Your faith community. Are you genuinely connected, or just attending?
- Mentors and guides. Who has walked the path you are on and could share wisdom?
- Those you are guiding. Who might God be calling you to help navigate?

The Family Legacy of Navigation

As I write this, dealing with pancreatic cancer and chemotherapy, I am more grateful than ever for the relational navigation network God has built through our family. Eight grandchildren who all love the Lord, children who have become spiritual leaders, and a wife who has been my compass for over six decades, this is the true treasure of finding steady orientation through relationships.

When I am gone, they will continue to navigate by the same North Star, use the Bible as their map, and be guided by the same Spirit. But they will also have each other as navigation aids and can check their bearings against a community of faith that spans generations.

That is the ultimate purpose of relational navigation: not just finding your own way, but creating a network of guides who help others find theirs. We are all both followers and leaders, all receiving help and giving it, all part of God's vast navigation system for His people.

A Prayer for Relational Navigation

Lord, thank You for not leaving me to find my way alone. Thank You for Tami, who helped me see You when I did not even know to look. Thank You for every person You have used to redirect my path: mentors, friends, children, even difficult people who taught me through challenges. Help me recognize the navigation aids You are providing today. Show me who needs my help finding their way. Keep all my relationships pointed toward You as our True North. Amen.

Coming Up Next...

Relationships can redirect our compass, but what about our daily work? How do we find North in our careers, especially when God seems to guide us through closed doors and unexpected turns? In the next chapter, we will explore finding purpose beyond the paycheck and discovering how God uses our professional lives as part of His navigation system.

Chapter 9

Finding North in Your Career

 Whatever you do, work heartily, as for the Lord and not
for men.

— Colossians 3:23

Careers rarely unfold in straight lines. More often they feel
like winding paths, full of detours, closed doors, and
surprising turns that only make sense in hindsight. What
seems like wandering is often God's way of weaving together preparation, character, and calling into a map far more intricate than anything
we could draft ourselves. Looking back, I see how each assignment,
whether mapping terrain in Vietnam, commanding a missile crew
underground, briefing senior leaders at the Pentagon, or mentoring
younger analysts as a contractor, was not wasted. Each was a training
ground. The Master Cartographer navigated my life to each location
and charted a course I could not have planned but that led me exactly
where He wanted me to go.

The Winding Path of Purpose

If I turn around and trace the course of my career, I see a map filled
with switchbacks, unexpected intersections, and roads that seemed to
end, only to bend toward something new. Each change felt like a

disruption. Now the pattern looks more like a photograph coming to life in the developer's solution, slowly revealing design and clarity I could not see then. In that slow unveiling, God was teaching me to trust the image before there was clarity.

Every assignment that once seemed like a detour was in fact essential terrain:

- **Cartography (1967–1972)** gave me an obsession with precision and orientation, teaching me that details matter and that even a one-degree error can change the course entirely.
- **Missile duty (1973–1977)** forged leadership under pressure and the humility to recover from failure, reminding me that every checklist, however routine, carries weight.
- **Intelligence work (1976–1985)** sharpened my eyes to patterns hidden beneath noise, training me in patience and discernment.
- **Pentagon service (1978–1988)** taught me how to navigate vast and complex human systems, where relationships and trust often mattered more than rank.
- **Contracting years (1988–2015)** showed me that one can still serve with excellence outside the uniform, mentoring the next generation and contributing from behind the scenes.

What once looked like a career full of wandering now appears as God's precise navigation. Each stage prepared me not only for the work itself, but for the person He was shaping me to become. Little by little, assignment by assignment, He was aligning my internal compass with His True North.

The Utah Rental: Learning to Wait

Not all of God's lessons came from jobs. Some came from everyday life.

When I deployed to Vietnam in 1971, Tami returned to Utah with our two small children, our daughter was five and our son almost four. Before leaving, we needed to find a short-term rental near her family in Salt Lake City. It turned out to be harder than we expected. The rental market was tight, university students had claimed most apartments, and a few landlords, upon learning we were not members of the predominant local faith, suddenly remembered that their properties were "already spoken for."

Then, in the middle of a December snowstorm that had dropped eight inches overnight, Tami noticed a hand-painted FOR RENT sign just up the road from her aunt's house. The paint was still fresh enough that the snow had not stuck to it. It could not have been there for more than a day.

The owners, a young Latter-day Saint couple who had recently returned from California where the husband had finished graduate school, were hesitant. They had hoped to rent to someone from their own ward, someone who shared their beliefs. But as they talked with Tami, her exhaustion showing, the children growing restless, snow still falling outside, something shifted. Maybe they saw a young mother doing her best, facing a year apart from her husband. Maybe God softened their hearts.

They agreed to rent us the top floor for a year, asking only that they could occasionally stop by for their family's traditional Monday "family home evening." Tami welcomed them warmly and kindly set a boundary that their visits would remain friendly rather than theological. And that is exactly how it went. Month after month, they showed kindness, fixing the heating when it failed, sharing vegetables from their garden, and even defending their decision to skeptical neighbors who wondered why they had rented to outsiders.

That year became a lasting reminder of how God's timing works. What looked impossible, finding a place to live in a snowstorm with two small children and a soon-to-be-deployed husband, was resolved at the exact moment it needed to be. It was as if God whispered again, "Be patient. Stop trying to force doors open. I am already preparing the right one."

That rental became a parable for my entire working life. When career doors slammed shut, and they did many times, God reminded me that the right one would open on His timeline. Not early. Rarely when I wanted it. But always exactly when it was needed.

When God Closes Doors

In 1972, the Air Force made a decision that upended my carefully planned career. They transferred all cartographic units to the newly formed Defense Mapping Agency, effectively civilianizing the positions. After five years of making maps that guided everything from supply flights to combat missions, my job disappeared overnight. The specialty I had trained for, excelled in, and built my identity around suddenly gone because of a bureaucratic reorganization.

The door I had walked through so confidently as a young lieutenant was not just closing, it was being sealed shut. I remember sitting in my office at March Air Force Base, surrounded by maps that represented hundreds of hours of careful work, and wondering if I had wasted five years of my life.

I could have fought the decision, tried to transfer to the new civilian agency, and clung to what I knew. Instead, I made a phone call to Tom Neary, the friend from my unit in California who had recently transferred to the missile field.

"If you want something different," he said, his voice crackling through the long-distance line, "I can get you into ICBM training. It's not glamorous, you'll be sitting underground in North Dakota or Montana, but it's important work, and they need people who pay attention to details."

From making maps to manning missiles. It made no sense on paper, but that pivot became one of the most formative seasons of my life. Missile duty taught me leadership under pressure, composure in monotony, and the discipline of accountability. It reminded me that true character is revealed in the long, quiet stretches when no one is watching.

That role also gave me opportunities I never expected, commanding crews, training others, evaluating performance, and learning to lead without losing humility.

I resonated with Paul's proclamation about contentment when he said, "I have learned the secret of being content in any and every situation, whether well fed or hungry, whether living in plenty or in want" (Phil 4:12 NIV). Paul's life as a traveling evangelist led him to all types of situations and I've been challenged by his ability to find peace. He even shared his secret being that he could do it all "through him who gives me strength." (Phil 4:13 NIV).

Even though that career change felt forced at the time, I recognize that God wasn't closing doors as a way to punish me. He was rerouting me toward a deeper purpose. It started with being able to find peace even in difficult times.

The Booz Allen Transformation

After twenty-one years in the Air Force, I stood at another crossroads. The military offered me two options: retire as a lieutenant colonel or accept reassignment back into cartography. Ironically, even though this was the same field I had been forced to leave more than a decade earlier, the field had evolved so much, and I had changed, so it didn't appeal to me in the same way. At that point, computers had replaced much of what we once did by hand. The choice seemed obvious when looking at it from face value. All signs pointed that I should retire with honor, secure a pension, and stop moving every few years.

But something inside me was not ready to stop serving. I was only forty-three. I still had energy, skills, and a deep desire to contribute. The calling to serve my country had not expired just because the uniform would. So, I traded my military ID for a contractor badge and joined Booz Allen Hamilton, one of the nation's premier consulting firms for defense and intelligence.

At first, the shift was jarring. I went from commanding crews and briefing generals to sitting in conference rooms filled with analysts, strategists, and engineers. The culture was different, the structure looser, the language more corporate than military. I found myself trying to fit the discipline of an officer into the rhythm of consultants who worked in subtler, more political ways.

For the first ten years, I was competent but uninspired. My work was solid and my performance reviews strong, but I felt like a man flying on instruments with no visual horizon. I supported major programs, but there was no spark, no sense of inner purpose. Looking back, I now realize those years were preparation. God was teaching me to be faithful in the middle chapters, to work with excellence even when the assignment did not feel meaningful.

This is when that phone call I described earlier happened. It was

1998 and my colleague from another division said, "Tom, we need someone with your exact background—cartography, missiles, intelligence, and especially your clearances—for a tough client. Can you come to Arlington for a meeting?"

As I've noted, that one call changed the course of my career. What I thought would be a short-term troubleshooting assignment turned into seventeen years of deeply satisfying work. I was placed in a division supporting a research agency whose mission was both complex and vital. It was the kind of work that tested every skill I had ever learned. Within two years, I was promoted to senior associate and leading a team of biologists, analysts, and engineers on projects critical to national security.

I cannot discuss the details of that work, but I can tell you this, it was the culmination of everything God had been preparing me for. Every previous assignment suddenly made sense. The precision from my mapping days helped me manage intricate data systems. The composure learned in missile duty steadied me during crises. The analytical patience from intelligence work helped me interpret complex reports. Even the leadership skills from the Pentagon allowed me to navigate bureaucratic challenges with wisdom rather than frustration.

I believe the Master Cartographer had been patiently drawing the connections all along, and that was the opportunity to see how perfectly they aligned.

Mentors and friendships along the way were major tools that God used to shape my path. I've described a few already. Ed Brezeale is another example of a friendship that had begun years earlier at the Air War College. Later, when Ed was stationed in Europe, he ended up staying with Tom Neary's family while waiting for his own to arrive. That connection led to opportunities and introductions that would later influence my civilian career. None of it was coincidence. These were divine appointments, relationships that became coordinates on the map of God's faithfulness.

The Booz Allen years redefined what success meant to me. Advancement and salary mattered, but they were no longer the goal. The true reward came in mentoring younger analysts, seeing them grow in confidence and integrity, and knowing that my underlying faith shaped the culture of our team.

There were days when I sensed God's presence in the smallest details, guiding meetings, providing words at just the right time, and opening hearts in ways that even my best strategizing never could. I began to see that faith in the workplace was not necessarily about direct evangelizing, but about embodying excellence, humility, and reliability that a relationship with Christ brings. My prayer each morning became simple: *Lord, help me represent You well today.*

Purpose Beyond the Paycheck

The Old Testament telling of Joseph and his rise to become the second-in-command of Egypt demonstrates how God shapes our paths. He orchestrates our training and life-circumstances to prepare us in advance for specific seasons and situations where those past experiences will be crucial to draw strength from.

God put Joseph in the position to become second-in-command of Egypt not for Joseph to receive glory but to save nations from famine, especially God's chosen people. Joseph endured and remained faithful through difficult circumstances, and His promotion to Pharaoh's assistant was the culmination of a series of assignments that looked, at first glance, like tragedies. His brothers sold him into slavery. He was falsely accused and thrown into prison. He was forgotten by those he helped. Yet in every dark place, Joseph kept doing what was in front of him with integrity, faithfulness, and excellence. When the time came, God elevated him to a position that required every skill and every lesson forged in those years when it seemed he had been abandoned.

As I consider the life of Joseph, it's clear to me that the purpose of a career is never just to make a living. It is to join God in the larger work He is doing in the world. Our day-to-day jobs may change, the environments may shift, but the calling remains: to serve, to grow, and to bear witness to His character wherever we are placed.

My years at Booz Allen were never about climbing a corporate ladder. The work became a ministry and each day I tried to stay faithful to the task before me, mentoring those entrusted to my care, and doing my work with excellence as an act of worship. Promotion and recognition were of course welcomed when they came, but they were not the goal. My frame of reference was God and working in a way that would please Him even if no one else noticed.

Scripture is filled with people who used their talents and skills in secular "day jobs" while remaining committed to following God's lead in whatever position He brought them. These "tentmakers" were missionaries in disguise.

- Paul was a tentmaker (Acts 18:3) which is where we get the word used to describe this occupation. His hands made tents while his heart and mind stayed fixed on spreading the Good News of the Gospel and encouraging members of the early church. the gospel. His tentmaking work provided resources for his daily needs, but more importantly gave him a connection for relating and building friendships with those he came into contact with.
- Daniel served foreign kings who worshiped idols. While it wasn't Daniel's choice to remain in exile as a servant, he maintained integrity and lived a life that pointed to Yahweh. Daniel refused to compromise truth and his commitment to God was surely a testimony to those around him.

Both Paul and Daniel understood something we often forget: excellence in ordinary work is not separate from faith. It is faith in motion. God's name is honored when His people do their daily labor with precision, honesty, and care.

That realization changed how I saw my own professional world. I began to recognize that my career was not separate from my calling. The intelligence reports I reviewed, and the briefings I delivered were all opportunities to reflect the God who values order, truth, and excellence.

At one time I might have thought serving God required standing behind a pulpit on Sunday mornings, but over time I came to see that my pulpit was often a conference table, my congregation a team of analysts or military officers, and my sermons the quiet example of integrity, patience, and competence in a field where shortcuts were common.

My coworkers knew that I would not compromise accuracy to please a client or soften an analysis for politics. They knew they could trust my word. In time, that consistency became its own witness.

Mentorship also became a form of discipleship. Younger professionals didn't just need technical coaching; they needed someone to remind them that their work mattered to God. Many of them had never considered that the way they handled data, deadlines, or office politics could reveal the character of Christ. When I saw that realization dawn on them, it confirmed something vital: the workplace can be one of the most strategic mission fields in the world.

Serving with excellence, integrity, and humility sanctifies ordinary labor. It turns routine into devotion and deadlines into opportunities for grace. Over time I learned that success is not measured by salary, title, or influence, but by the degree to which our work reflects the heart of God. To show up fully, to give your best effort, to serve others through your craft; that is worship.

When I look back now, I see that every season of work, from the underground missile capsule to the Pentagon briefing room, was ministry. The uniforms changed, but the purpose stayed constant. I was there to serve God by serving people.

Navigation Callout: The Northwest Passage Obsession

For more than four centuries, explorers searched for a Northwest Passage through the Arctic, a shortcut from Europe to Asia that would bypass the long and dangerous voyage around South America. Convinced by logic, ambition, and national pride that such a route must exist, expedition after expedition vanished into the ice. Their quests for easy access to the riches of Asia were slowed by a host of challenges including sea ice, harsh weather, and also navigational challenges.

In 1845, Sir John Franklin set off on one such expedition that would become the most famous of these doomed ventures. Two ships and 129 men never returned. The sunken ships were not discovered until 2014 and 2016. The tragedy was not only in their deaths but in their dependence on maps that were outdated in their indication that a water passage existed where it did not. The ships became trapped in ice because of maps that led them to believe there was a clever way through.

The story has haunted historians, but it has also become a parable for me. We often do the same in our careers. We chase shortcuts that promise quick advancement. It's easy to mistake recognition for progress and sometimes this leads to positions we never wanted to be in.

Sometimes God must redirect us to what feels like the long way around —the route around the Cape of Good Hope instead of through the ice.

That path is longer, slower, and often humbling. Yet it is navigable. It gets us to the destination alive and equipped for what lies ahead. Along the way, the detour becomes an opportunity for growth.

In reality, those who first understood the Northwest Passage are the Inuit. Over generations, their traditional knowledge was shared and they avoided the dangerous places while understanding how to survive in the wilderness. They understood the terrain and didn't push a route that simply was impassable. When European explorers began to respect the ice and learn from the Inuit, they too made the passage successfully. In doing so, they discovered that survival depended not on pride but on humility, the willingness to learn, to listen, and to follow knowledge of those who knew best.

Our careers require that same humility. Sometimes success means learning from those we once overlooked, listening to unexpected mentors, and allowing God to redraw the route. Faith means trusting that even when the way feels slow or uncertain, the Master Navigator knows what conditions we are ready for and which passages remain impassable for now.

Navigating Your Own Career

Look back at your professional path. What do you see? Random jobs or divine preparation? Closed doors or divine redirection? Seasons of frustration or foundations being laid for a future you could not yet see?

I've learned a lot from my four decades of wandering through a variety of careers. So many times, I thought I knew the best path only to have God redirect my way. Even though those obstacles felt like interruptions, I do understand now that God knew the route and He never gets lost even when we feel disoriented.

Because we don't know for what reason He has placed us in a given situation, and because I've learned to work for the glory of God, not for man, I always strive for excellence. Just as Joseph worked faithfully in Potiphar's house before entering Pharaoh's palace and Daniel remained committed to Yahweh and his standards, I've come to understand the importance of doing my best wherever I am. Excellence opens doors to new destinations.

For me, the new doors have been opportunities I wouldn't have imagined for myself and they've often come through unexpected relationships and conversations. Whether a casual conversation in the hall-way, an unexpected email, or a colleague who calls out of the blue, divine appointments rarely appear life-changing until the Holy Spirit starts tugging on our hearts. Pay attention. God's direction often arrives wearing ordinary clothes.

When I was twenty-two, I had my career mapped out in ink. None of it happened the way I expected, and that turned out to be grace. My plans were short-sided and I may have settled into monotony without knowing a way to get out. But God's plan led to opportunities to provide influence, mentorship, and purpose that reached further than I imagined.

God's plan is to put you on mission, to be used by Him in places unlikely to be in our plans when we start out. It may be that your mission field ends up as your cubicle, your classroom, your kitchen, or your shop floor. Wherever you find yourself working, do not wait for the "real" calling to start serving God. Ministry happens wherever His people show up with integrity and joy.

I never imagined that one day I would write a book about the path God put me on, but as I look back, I'm grateful for all of the notes I kept on God's faithfulness. Our faith can be strengthened when we pause to write down the God moments of our lives, those specific instances when the right opportunity appeared at the exact time it was needed. Over the years, you will see the threads connect into a story that could not have been written by chance.

The View from Retirement

Now, standing at the vantage point of retirement, I have a clear picture of the map God used to guide my life. I smile to think about the ways so circumstances that didn't make sense in the moment now fit as guides that brought me to where I am today. Every assignment, every failure, every unexpected turn was precisely placed. The boy who once built model airplanes and studied maps became a man who learned to trust the One who writes the larger story.

It's fascinating to realize that the best turns God took me through in terms of my career were not necessarily the ones that came with the most lofty title or highest salary. Years ago, a Pentagon supervisor told me that careers are more like weather systems than topographic maps.

He was partly right. The patterns shift, the winds change, and forecasts are uncertain. But what he missed was the most important truth: there is a Master Meteorologist who sees every pattern, understands every pressure system, and guides His people through each storm. Our task is not to predict the weather but to adjust our sails and trust the One who commands the wind.

Reflection and Application

- **Reflect:** Think of a career setback or closed door you've experienced. How might God have used it as a redirection?
- **Act:** Invite God into your work this week. Pray before a meeting, or intentionally encourage a colleague. Small choices re-orient us toward True North.
- **Practice Patience:** If a door has closed, don't panic. Ask God to show you the next step, even if it's just a "For Rent" sign in a snowstorm.
- **Pray:** *Lord, show me Your map for my career. Help me trust Your detours, wait with patience, and work with purpose. Amen.*

A Prayer for Professional Navigation

Lord, I surrender my career plans to Your perfect navigation. Help me work with excellence wherever You place me, knowing that ultimately I'm working for You, not human bosses or organizations. Open my eyes to the divine appointments hidden in ordinary interactions. Give me courage to walk through new doors when You close old ones, even when I can't see where they lead. Help me trust that every assignment, every setback, every unexpected turn is part of Your preparation. May my work, whatever it is, point others to You. When I'm tempted to force doors open or cling to positions You're calling me to leave, remind me of Your faithfulness in the past. Help me hold my plans loosely and Your purposes tightly. In Jesus' name, Amen.

Coming Up Next...

My career taught me to trust God's map through unexpected pivots, like Joseph's rise from the pit his brothers tried to abandon him to the palace where he was second in command. But what happens when the map leads through failure? In Chapter 10, "Finding North Through Failure," we'll explore how setbacks, like my fall from the roof or Peter's denial of Jesus, aren't dead ends but God's way of reorienting us. Using the Bible as our compass, we'll see God's grace turns failures into new paths toward His purpose.

Chapter 10

Finding North Through Failure
When Your Compass Spins Wildly

 For from his fullness we have all received, grace upon grace.

— John 1:16

It was either late November or early December of 1973 in Montana where the cold months blur together into a single frozen landscape. I've mentioned this experience earlier and want to elaborate on it more here. I stood in the Wing Commander's office at Malmstrom Air Force Base, certain that I had just watched my Air Force career sink beneath the ice.

An evaluation team had failed me during a launch control exercise in the missile capsule ninety feet underground. The verdict came quickly: I was to be demoted from crew commander to deputy. Six years into my Air Force career, I felt like a complete failure.

I can still remember the sterile room, the sound of the door closing behind me, and the hollow feeling that followed. For years I had built my identity around things the military values like precision, reliability, and competence. Suddenly, all of that seemed to vanish in a single failure.

At the time, I saw only humiliation. What I could not see was that this would become one of God's most precise course corrections. The failure was not the end of my map. It was a forced turn and God, my True North was guiding every step of the way.

The Missile Crisis: Demotion and the Gift of Mentors

Within days of my demotion, the Air Force assigned me to retrain under seasoned, battle-tested crews. It felt like a punishment at first, but it turned out to be grace in disguise.

I quoted my senior officer in a previous chapter who watched me stumble through a complex missile scenario and quietly told me to trust the procedures and stop trying to outsmart the system.

His advice sounded simple enough, but it took humility to accept. I had been overthinking every move, afraid of making another mistake. I wanted to prove myself, but what I really needed was to relearn trust in the system, trust in the training, and ultimately trust in God's ability to guide through disciplined routines as well as in the moment feelings.

As I've described earlier, I grew in those weeks of drills. My confidence was restored and I gained a deep respect for those who trained me with patience yet firmness. They didn't minimize my failure, it was crucial for me to know the process completely, but they did not grow weary in helping me navigate through it.

Within a few months, I was restored to crew commander and paired with a deputy who shared my steady temperament. We ran hundreds of drills together, and slowly, my confidence, and competence grew and by the following year, I was selected as an instructor. Then a year later, an evaluator. All of this happened as a lead-up to the time when I represented the wing at Olympic Arena, the premier missile competition in the Air Force. Despite our initial poor performance, we came back the following year and nearly swept the awards. From feeling like my career was over to being a representative of the wing in three years, I knew only God could write a story like that.

Stories of Redemption

The Bible is full of people who went through a journey of failure and redemption. The fact that God uses broken people is one of the most amazing and inspiring aspects of humanity. There was Jonah who failed in a big way by not obeying God and going to Ninevah to warn the people there of God's impending judgement. God used Jonah anyway even though it required a violent stormy sea and three nights in the belly of a great fish. It's humorous that even though he desperately tried, Jonah could not get himself off of the path God had for him.

Peter is another example of redemption in the Bible. He had promised Jesus that even if everyone else fell away, he never would. He was bold, loud, and sure of himself, until the moment when fear cut through his confidence. Three denials later, a rooster crowed and Peter's certainty shattered.

But Jesus was not finished with him. After the resurrection, beside the Sea of Galilee, Jesus met Peter again and over a charcoal fire, like the one where Peter had once denied Him, Jesus asked three questions that pierced and healed Peter all at the same time. "Do you love me?" He asked. And three times Peter answered yes. Then came Jesus' commission and evidence of forgiveness and redemption: "Feed my sheep."

That is how God restores people. He does not pretend the failure never happened, and He does not erase the memory. Rather, He transforms us and our failures into opportunities to grow in a deeper understanding of grace.

Being on those missile crews and having opportunities to participate in the missile competitions were my chance to practice faithfulness where I had once faltered. With each success, my confidence was rebuilt and my heart was renewed.

Failure, I discovered, is not the end of the story. It is often the first honest chapter. God uses it to break open what pride once sealed, and then He fills that space with strength that is no longer self-made. Wherever it happens, the pattern is the same. Grace finds us when we start listening.

The Roof Fall: Power Perfected in Weakness

In the months after that storm when I climbed on the roof to replace a set of floodlights and fell hard onto the concrete below, I could not drive, dress, or lift anything heavier than a glass of water. Tami became my hands and sometimes my strength of will. Our children turned into my encouragers, their humor lightening what could have been a season of despair.

My supervisor at Booz Allen, Norma Barnett, showed extraordinary kindness. She told me to take the time I needed to heal and promised that my place would be waiting. Her compassion allowed me to return to work gradually, with dignity and gratitude rather than guilt.

The forced dependence of that season brought an unexpected intimacy to our home. We had to slow down and talk more. We prayed together, read together, and shared small victories over simple things like when I climbed the stairs without help. It reminded me how much I had taken for granted.

Again, my patience was challenged in wanting to rush ahead of God's timeline especially in regards to the return of my strength, healing, and what I believed to be my control. God's grace in that season came exactly because of my limitations. I learned to receive kindness and help from the doctors who adjusted my brace, the coworkers who covered my workload, and friends who brought meals and refused to let me wallow. Each act of care taught me the humility of receiving and being grateful that God had placed people demonstrating kindness into my life.

The Apostle Paul wrote, "My grace is sufficient for you, for my power is made perfect in weakness" (2 Corinthians 12:9). I had quoted that verse many times in Bible studies and conversations, but during that long recovery it finally became personal. God's strength does not simply replace ours; it flows through our weakness, redeeming it from the inside out.

That fall on the asphalt broke nothing essential. It actually brought opportunities for God to build in me characteristics I had long struggled to live out: patience, gratitude, humility, and trust. I had once thought strength meant self-sufficiency, but learned that real strength is found in relying on God's provision.

God's Grace in the Wreckage

In his letter to the Corinthians, Paul wrote about a thorn in his flesh. He described how this unwelcome presence in his life brought a new understanding about God's power. As 2 Corinthians 12:9 demonstrates, Paul's thorn taught him to boast in weakness. In my time of healing after my back injury, I joined Paul in understanding God's sufficient grace and His great power.

When you cannot bend, lift, or even open a jar, life slows and every small task becomes an opportunity for patience and humility. Before that season, I believed excellence meant independence. My worth seemed tied to performance, to solving problems, and to staying in control. When my body which had carried me through years of military discipline refused to cooperate, I learned that true strength is about offering ourselves back to the One who gave me abilities in the first place.

Grace did not erase the difficulty of the season after my fall, but it did build something in my life that made it better than it had been before. Through God's power I grew in endurance, faith, and unexpectedly, peace. Looking back, I can see that the fall was not an accident. It was a holy interruption that exposed the limits of my own strength and revealed the sufficiency of God's. His grace was not merely enough. It was abundant.

Navigation Callout: Wrong Way Corrigan

In 1938, Douglas "Wrong Way" Corrigan became famous for one of history's most winked at navigational "mistakes." Corrigan flew his plane, which had been rescued from an airplane junkyard, from California to New York. He had hoped to fly onward across the Atlantic, but once in New York, the plane was deemed not safe enough to make the transatlantic trip. Supposedly submitting to the decision, Corrigan filed a flight plan to return to California.

What happened next surprised everyone, except Corrigan, who likely knew exactly what he was doing. His plane took off westbound, but once in the air, did a 180-degree turn to head out over the Atlantic and into a bank of clouds. After 27 hours of flying, Corrigan stepped out of his plane and reportedly said, "Just got in from New York. Where am I?" In fact he had landed in Dublin, Ireland. When officials asked how on earth he had crossed the Atlantic without authorization, he shrugged and said that his compass must have malfunctioned.

Most people suspected otherwise. Corrigan had been trying for years to obtain a permit for a transatlantic flight, but the aviation authorities repeatedly denied his requests. His so-called mistake accomplished what official channels had refused to allow. Reporters loved it. Crowds cheered him as he returned to America. His self-claimed error became his triumph.

There may not be many people who believe it really was a wrong turn, least of all Corrigan himself. Perhaps Corrigan had simply taken a creative route to fulfill the dream he believed was his calling.

Sometimes what looks like failure is not failure at all. It is an unconventional path to a desired outcome. If indeed Corrigan did intend to fly over the Atlantic, he didn't fail and wasn't surprised by the destination. Our lives can follow a similar pattern. God never fails and He is never surprised by our destination, even though we might find ourselves led to a place we never intended. Like Corrigan, it may look like we have flown the "wrong way," but we arrive exactly where we are meant to be.

Navigation Practice: Failure Cartography

In this chapter we've looked at my failures, biblical failures, and even the supposed failure of Wrong Way Corrigan. Although it's a sad truth, if you live long enough, failure will be part of your journey. The good news is that just as God has used failures in the past, He will continue to use them for purpose in your life.

It's not healthy to dwell long on our mistakes, but I encourage you to bravely look at your past and map out places where you have failed, where others have failed you, or even where it seems God has failed you. Don't spend too much time rehearsing all of the "if onlys" and "should haves." The past is what it is.

At the same time, we can look for God's hand even in what seemed to be failures. Trace God's hand through the experiences. Do you see the condition of your heart before the failure, during, and after. As you look back, do you see a trail coming into focus of where God was redirecting you, perhaps even keeping you from a place of danger or protecting you from an unknown hurt. Look at where you ended up and see the growth God developed in you through the times of failure.

If you're in the middle of a recent failure, be encouraged. You are not alone. We all make mistakes, fail, and maybe even land flat on our backs as I did. God is not done in your journey and will never abandon you. Even in this very difficult time God sees you and He is preparing you for a future far better than you can imagine.

Reflection and Application

- **Reflect:** Name one failure that still stings. Where do you now see God's preserving grace?
- **Act:** Tell the story to a trusted friend, emphasizing God's redirection more than your regret.
- **Mentor:** Offer someone the kind of patient encouragement and challenge you received.
- **Pray:** *Lord, meet me in my failure. Like Peter, restore me; like David, cleanse me; like Paul, strengthen me; like Jonah, redirect me. Amen.*

Coming Up Next...

We've traced God's hand through detours and wreckage. In the next chapter, we'll chart how resilient hope forms over decades—how to cultivate a compass that holds when storms return.

Chapter 11

Finding North in Physical Trials

 And we know that for those who love God all things work together for good, for those who are called according to his purpose.

— Romans 8:28

During my recovery from the fall, I came face to face with an understanding that physical trials strip away illusions. They remind us that the body is not just a vehicle for work and accomplishing career goals, but more than that our bodies are tools through which God demonstrates His grace. Our injuries and illnesses are reminders to submit to God and learn to depend on Him more. I once thought faith was mostly about spiritual resilience, but pain taught me that faith goes deeper through every breath. God is strong to meet our needs and when we need help to do ordinary tasks, we are able to see the way He's always working.

There is a strange mercy in being slowed down. When your body insists on rest, you notice things you once rushed past: the sound of wind in the trees, your spouse's patience, the way a friend's visit feels like water to dry ground. Suffering rewires your attention and if we're listening , our questions of "Why me?" turn into "What now, Lord?"

When Your Body Becomes Your Teacher

For most of my adult life, my body had been a tool, something I used to accomplish tasks. Air Force training, physical fitness tests, home repairs —I expected my body to perform on command. I never really examined that relationship until it broke down.

During my recovery, even simple tasks required help. My body that had always served me effortlessly without question then dictated the terms of how each day would unfold. My wife Tami and our children helped with nearly everything. All of their acts of care and patient gestures taught me more about grace than any leadership seminar or military training ever had.

This reversal, from commanding my body to submitting to its limits, revealed truths that I never would have learned if my strength had not been taken away. Our culture celebrates toughness and grit, but what happens when you simply cannot push through? In the moments when our efforts can no longer solve the problems, that's when God has our attention and our faith is most likely to mature. Those are the scenarios when the Apostle Paul's words, "My power is made perfect in weakness," stop sounding poetic and start sounding practical.

When you cannot open a jar, lift a box, or walk unassisted, you begin to understand grace in new dimensions. In my physically defeated position, I saw that my body's physical weakness forced my gaze to turn upward.

Jacob's Profitable Limp

My back never fully recovered from the fall. I wouldn't wish to go through the fall and healing process again, but now I carry this reminder of God's strength in my weakness every day. The biblical account of Jacob wrestling at the Jabbok River in Genesis 32 tells us that he too carried a reminder of God's will for his life. Jacob wrestled all night with a mysterious figure who turned out to be God Himself. At dawn, his opponent touched his hip socket, dislocating it. From that night forward, Jacob would walk with a limp.

During the night time wrestling match, Jacob would not let go. Even though he was outmatched, he held on and demanded a blessing. "I will not let you go unless you bless me" (verse 26). God granted the blessing, but it came with both a cost and a calling. Jacob received a new name, Israel, which means "one who strives with God." The wound and the blessing arrived together, inseparable.

Even now, decades later, my back aches from time to time, especially when I push myself too hard. Yet I would not trade this limitation for my old strength. The ache is a reminder that God never stops using to keep me connected to Him for the journey. Every morning I am forced to remember that I am not self-sufficient, that I need grace, that I am still learning to rely on others and on God. For someone wired to lead, to plan, and to stay in control, that reminder has become one of God's greatest mercies.

The Technology of Limitation

During those months of recovery, I began to notice something I now call "the technology of limitation." It is the way God uses restriction as a tool for growth. I certainly did not see it that way at first. Pain felt like interruption, not instruction. But over time I realized that limitation, handled with humility, can become a kind of sacred technology, an instrument through which God rewires our attention and reorders our hearts.

Physical pain anchors you in the present moment. You cannot plan too far ahead when today's pain demands your full attention. That forced presence can become a spiritual discipline. When the body slows you down, the soul finally catches up.

As I needed help with ordinary tasks my relationships with others deepened. Dismantled along with my self reliance was my pride. However, that weakness forged bonds that wouldn't have formed if my strength had remained intact. In the military, I had learned to lead from competence. In recovery, I learned to lead from vulnerability, and surprisingly kind of leadership has a deeper reach.

When everything slowed down I noticed what had been hidden in the blur of busyness: the patience of my wife, the loyalty of friends, the never-ending kindness of God. Even the smell of morning coffee or the light through a window became a motivation for my gratitude.

At first I found that asking for help was harder than any missile simulation, field test, or evaluation I ever faced. But it built a different kind of strength, the strength to receive without embarrassment, to thank without pride, and to rest without guilt. That strength, I have come to believe, is what Scripture means when it says, "My power is made perfect in weakness."

The Cancer Classroom

Even though I understand that a cancer diagnosis is not a personal failure, I couldn't help but see it as a blow to my personal strength when in 2025, I was diagnosed with pancreatic cancer. There was a tumor on my pancreas, confirmed malignant after biopsy. The surgery, an eleven-hour Whipple procedure, removed the head of my pancreas, part of my stomach, my duodenum, and my gallbladder, which the surgeon said looked like a rock.

When the pathology results showed cancer in several lymph nodes, we knew it had spread. Chemotherapy would be necessary. Another physical trial, another class I hadn't enrolled in voluntarily.

But this time, I recognized the curriculum. The lessons I learned from the roof fall had prepared me for this more profound physical challenge. I knew how to be dependent. I knew how to receive help. I understood that physical limitation didn't mean spiritual limitation.

Chemotherapy brought its own teachings. They centered around understanding how to see God even in intense fatigue, neuropathy, and having to carefully manage good days and bad days. Yet in this physical trial, I'm discovering depths of grace I hadn't known existed. When Tami helps me, when friends from church bring meals—these aren't just isolated acts of kindness. Their help is the body of Christ functioning as designed.

Navigation Callout: Shackleton's Miraculous Navigation

In 1914, Sir Ernest Shackleton and his crew of 27 men set out in the ship Endurance to be the first to cross Antarctica from one side to the other. Endurance became trapped in ice for nearly a year and eventually was crushed in the Antarctic ice in 1915. Forced to abandon the ship, the crew camped on the ice, hoping they would drift close to an island. However, by April 1916, it became apparent that they would need to take further action to be rescued. They sailed in the three ships from Endurance and eventually reached Elephant Island.

Again, it became evident this island was incredibly remote and they would need to seek out further help. Shackleton and five other men then set off across the most dangerous seas on Earth in a 22-foot lifeboat, the James Caird, to reach help.

Their passage and navigation accuracy are nearly miraculous. The crew navigated 800 miles of the most dangerous seas on Earth in a 22-foot lifeboat to reach South Georgia Island. Using only a sextant, dead reckoning, and occasional sun sights through clouds, Shackleton and his navigator, Frank Worsley, hit their target despite hurricane-strength winds and having to bail water from the boat around the clock.

Navigation aboard the James Caird was a challenge to say the least. Not only did the weather not cooperate by remaining covered in clouds, but the ability to take accurate sextant readings was challenged. The boat was small for the six men and their supplies, leaving little room to maneuver and take accurate readings and the towering continuous waves left few opportunities to obtain good measurements based on the horizon.

The navigation skills of Worsley and Shackleton in spite of difficult conditions and fewer tools made the journey successful. When we come to the end of our own resources and are forced to rely on God's grace and guidance to navigate, our eyes are opened to His provision and strength in ways we may not have uncovered during times of comfort.

Shackleton's story resonates with my experience of physical trials and maybe you have experienced the same. When our bodies break, when cancer arrives, when limitations multiply—we discover different ways to navigate life. Often this comes through a new awareness of our dependence on God and the Body of Christ to help us find our way.

The Intimacy of Illness

There have been many unexpected discoveries along my cancer journey. One of the best has been a revelation that I believe applies to all physical trials, not just cancer. In this illness, the intimacy in my marriage has deepened in amazing ways. Tami and I have been married since 1964. We have always had a good marriage built on respect, humor, and shared faith. Yet military life shaped both of us into people who valued independence. I was trained to handle crises, to lead under pressure, and to stay composed. She was trained, by years of deployments and separations, to manage life when I was away. We learned to stand strong, sometimes side by side, sometimes apart.

Cancer changed all of that. Now we are facing mortality together, and like when I fell off the roof, I've needed to depend on Tami for my basic needs. In moments of crisis like this, illusions of control fade away. The careful distances that once protected our independence dissolve in the face of vulnerability. What had once been a partnership of two capable people became something more intimate, more raw, and more sacred.

The details of caregiving are not what matters most. What matters is the way God can use these ordinary acts of care to deepen our relationship with Him. All of a sudden, I'm aware of the way ordinary acts of care like helping with medication, preparing meals, and sitting through long silences have become methods to receive and give grace. These circumstances could have been humiliating but by reframing our perspective, we see God's goodness in His provision. Illness has stripped away the unnecessary layers of self-sufficiency until only sacrificial love remains.

I have learned that dependency, when received in humility, is not weakness but a refining tool from God to see His character through the hands of another, through the kindness of a spouse who has borne with me when I can no longer bear my own weight. Tami's love during this season has been steadfast, gentle, and unflinching. It has reminded me that marriage is not only a covenant of companionship but a living parable of grace.

Paul's Pedagogical Thorn

Paul's "thorn in the flesh" remains one of Scripture's most enduring mysteries. Scholars have speculated for centuries about what it was, such as chronic pain, poor eyesight, depression, or opposition from enemies, but Paul never tells us. Perhaps the silence is deliberate. The specific nature of the thorn matters less than the divine purpose behind it.

Three times Paul begged God to remove the thorn. Instead of agreeing to remove the trial, God responded with those words that have become life-lines for every sufferer since: "My grace is sufficient for you, for my power is made perfect in weakness" (2 Corinthians 12:9). I've felt God's increasing provision in many ways throughout my life, especially through cancer and the lingering effects of my back injury. The thorn was not a punishment for Paul and I don't believe it is in my situation either. Rather, it's a reminder to remain dependent on God, connected to others, and aware of His grace.

When your body weakens, your prayers often simplify into a focus on the basics like, "Lord, help me through this day." "Thank You for one more morning." Those prayers, small as they sound, are the ones that may keep our perspective focused on God rather than our difficult situations. Grace often multiplies in the very places where our pain lingers.

Suffering has become, for me, not a detour from the spiritual journey but a deeper path into it. Weakness teaches lessons that strength cannot. It opens doors to compassion, honesty, and surrender and reveals that God's power is not the escape to avoid suffering but the ability to endure it with peace, faith, and love.

The Curriculum of the Body

I've talked a lot in this book about my fall from the roof and my journey with cancer. It's no accident that the most significant life lessons I have to share came through physical trials. I would never have learned these deep things of God through success or even studying in a classroom. It has taken long period of difficulty to grow in submission to His plan His roadmap for my journey.

We are integrated beings. What happens to the body affects the soul, and what happens to the soul affects the body. Healing is never just physical or just spiritual; it is both. God works in the whole person. When He restores one part, He inevitably touches the others.

Independence is largely an illusion that health allows us to maintain. As long as we are strong, we imagine ourselves to be self-sufficient. Physical trials strip away that illusion and reveal our fundamental interdependence with others and our absolute dependence on God.

Strength is not what I once believed it to be. I used to think of it as the power to push through difficulty by willpower or training. Now I understand strength as the courage to persevere through chemotherapy, the humility to ask for help without shame, and the intentional decision to maintain gratitude even when the pain refuses to subside.

The body records every trauma, every trial, every grace. Scars, soreness, fatigue, and frailty can all be used to bring back to our mind God's control over every situation. God operates on a far larger timeline than ours. It's one that stretches into eternity. These "light and momentary afflictions," as Paul calls them, are producing something that far outweighs all of our difficult situations. The body may bear the marks of struggle, but the soul is being formed into something more Christlike that will last into eternity.

The Fellowship of the Wounded

Another unexpected grace that I've learned through my physical trials is the blessing of finding a new community. This is a fellowship of travelers who is rarely gathered in one place but instantly recognizes one another. I'm talking about the connection of those who have faced or are currently facing serious illness or injury, those who have heard difficult diagnoses, endured long recoveries, or learned to live with pain that never fully goes away.

We recognize each other and communicate deeply through knowing glances exchanged in a hospital waiting room, by a nod of understanding when someone mentions chronic fatigue, by a smile of comfort that communicates more than words ever could. This fellowship does not depend on shared background or belief, but on shared vulnerability.

Before my fall, I unconsciously sorted people into categories: strong and weak, healthy and sick, capable and limited. That division seems almost laughable to me now. Everyone is carrying something. Everyone's body is teaching them lessons about fragility, patience, and hope. We are all students in this same school, though some of us simply enroll earlier than others.

When we turn our focus in the middle of suffering upward and outward, God opens our eyes to the work He wants to do. He has the power to use our trials to turn strangers into companions. Gaining an awareness that His plan is bigger than our own is the beginning of seeing that grace circulates most freely among the wounded. The ones who have lost much are often the quickest to offer comfort, the first to forgive others, and the most generous in love.

Your Body's Secret Curriculum

Even though I've walked a path of painful injury already, I understand now that some of those lessons were only half learned. My body is still teaching me.What might your body be trying to teach you? Where are you fighting limitations that might actually be invitations to deeper dependence on God?

We all want to be strong, to push through, to overcome. Even though we want to be independent, God shows that His strength becomes felt only when ours runs out. We want to keep busy, be productive, manage our own lives, but sometimes the most sacred progress happens when we learn to slow down and approach life one step at a time.

My body is more fragile than it has ever been. My back remains damaged. My organs have been altered. My energy rises and falls with treatment cycles. Yet in all this brokenness, I have discovered a new kind of wholeness.

This is the paradox of physical trials: They break us open so that grace can enter. In our weakness, God's presence becomes unmistakable. In our suffering, His strength becomes our song.

Coming Up Next...

When the stars are hidden and the map is hard to read we can learn to navigate through the storms when God seems absent, and find Him even in the darkness.

Part Four

Navigating Through Storms

Chapter 12

When Clouds Hide the Stars

Why, O Lord, do you stand far away? Why do you hide
yourself in times of trouble?

— Psalm 10:1

J anuary 4, 1971. I arrived in Saigon as an Air Force captain,
assigned to work for an Army lieutenant colonel. Even though we
arrived in a war zone, our housing was a hotel. Saigon was a
strange mix of normalcy and chaos. The hotel had been bombed
just a week before I arrived.

Walking into that damaged building, seeing the patched walls and
boarded windows, knowing that people had died there days earlier, I
was, to put it plainly, scared to death.

That first night, lying in a bed where someone might have died a
week ago, I realized something unfamiliar inside of me. It wasn't just
fear, though there was plenty of that, but it felt more like a kind of spiritual disorientation. I'm not the first soldier to look for God when
coming face to face with mortality. I, too, wondered where was God in
this? For years I had been going to church, saying prayers, believing in
His protection. But when bombs fell randomly, when death visited the
place where I slept before I even arrived, I had to wrestle with figuring
out what divine protection even meant?

I struggled with this question until my tour ended December 17, 1971. The reality of my faith didn't disappear, but the truths of God, the stars by which I had been navigating, became harder to trust in through the smoke and fear of war.

When God Feels Distant in Danger

My original position was eliminated shortly after I arrived, and they moved me to Tan Son Nhut Air Base, into a hooch, military slang for our basic living quarters. I became a photo interpreter, working with strategic and tactical reconnaissance photography. I was in charge of a unit, but worked for an alcoholic major who was, to put it mildly, unpleasant.

He did not appreciate me. Bossy and critical, he was the kind of commander who made every day feel like walking through a minefield even as we were literally surrounded by them. Here is where I can see God's hand now, though I could not then. Our office space was strategically located. The major sat in front of me, but his boss was also right there, and we were next to the commander's office. The proximity to higher leadership provided a buffer, a protection I did not recognize at the time.

I prayed constantly. Not beautiful or eloquent prayers, but desperate ones. "God, help me have peace. Get me through this day. Keep me safe." I worked every single day, seven days a week. Most Sundays I went to chapel services on base. But here is the truth: I was going through the motions. My prayers felt like they were bouncing off the chapel ceiling. The hymns were just words. Even the sermons might as well have been in a foreign language.

God felt distant even though it was a time I needed Him desperately. This is what I mean by navigating without visibility, when you cannot sense God's presence but you keep using the instruments anyway. The trusted avenues of prayer felt hopeless, but I prayed anyway. I didn't feel God at church, but I went anyway. The map of Scripture blurred into words on a page.

The Deeper Darkness of Uncertainty

Although the Vietnam period was dark, it wasn't my darkest spiritual season. That came later, ironically, when external circumstances were fine. There was a period I cannot pinpoint exactly when, but my children were grown, I was established in my career, and questions of my purpose haunted me. I wondered: What was my purpose? Why had God put me on this earth?

I loved the Lord. I was going to church. I was working and taking care of my family. But I felt a deep spiritual trepidation, an insecurity about who I was before God. I prayed about it constantly. "God, why am I here? What am I supposed to be doing?"

Nothing came up. Silence.

It is strange, isn't it? Maybe God feels more distant when everything is fine. When there are no bombs falling, no career crises, no health emergencies, sometimes that is when the clouds are thickest. Perhaps it is because we do not desperately need Him in those moments. Or maybe it is because we finally have time to ask the deeper questions, and the answers do not come as quickly as we would like.

This spiritual uncertainty lasted for years. During that time, I constantly felt like I wasn't doing enough, not fulfilling whatever purpose God had for me. Externally, my life looked successful and smooth, but internally I felt like I was drifting without a compass.

Then it finally dawned on me, gradually, not in a lightning bolt moment, that family was my purpose. Not in some vague or sentimental way, but specifically in building and nurturing the family God had given me. The clarity really started to come into focus when my kids began having children of their own. Seeing the fruit in their lives, watching them raise their own children in faith, I realized that God meant for me to invest deeply in my children and grandchildren.

Elijah's Cave and My Questions

I wasn't the first to ask those questions, and I won't be the last. The prophet Elijah knew something about spiritual darkness. After his dramatic victory over the prophets of Baal when fire literally fell from heaven, the drought ended, and God's power had been on full display, you would think he would be spiritually soaring. Instead, one threat from Queen Jezebel sent him running into the wilderness, collapsing under a broom tree, begging God to let him die.

 It is enough; now, O LORD, take away my life, for I am no better than my fathers.

— 1 Kings 19:4

This great prophet of God sat in a cave, convinced that God had abandoned him, that his mission had failed, that he was utterly alone.

I understand that cave. Not that I've ever lived the dramatic life of a prophet-on-the-run, but I do relate to the ordinary cave of spiritual uncertainty. The kind when you are doing all the right things—praying, attending church, serving your family—but feeling nothing and only hearing silence when asking God for direction.

God responded to Elijah's desperation by providing food, energy to get up and move for the next part of the journey. Then forty days later, when Elijah again felt alone and discouraged, God came near to him, not in the earthquake, wind, or fire, but the stillness, in a low whisper that the King James version calls "a still small voice."

In my long season of searching for God's presence, I looked for Him in spectacular moments when He was whispering in the ordinary. He didn't reveal His purpose for me n a dramatic vision or prophetic word. It was revealed in watching my grandchildren grow, in seeing my children's faith mature, in recognizing the legacy being built through ordinary faithfulness.

Navigating by Instruments Alone

There is a story that perfectly captures what I mean by spiritual instrument navigation. Tami and I were adult guest hosts at a Young Life camp near where the New York, New Jersey, and Pennsylvania borders all meet. When a busload of kids came into camp, some of them were having a pillow fight on the bus, and one student was hit in the eye by something solid. I volunteered to take him to a local doctor. The local doctor was worried about his retina and sent him by ambulance to a New York City clinic almost two hours away. I followed in my car.

After his treatment, his eye would recover, but on the drive back I suddenly ran into dense fog that made it nearly impossible to see out of the windshield. The weather was terrible, and it was the middle of the night.

But I had a map. Not GPS, this was before those days, but an actual paper map. I followed it methodically, exit by exit, mile by mile, barely able to see the road signs until I was right on top of them. We made it home safely, navigating entirely by trust in the map rather than by what I could see outside of the vehicle.

That is exactly what faith during dark seasons is like. You follow the map, God's Word, even when you can barely see it. You trust the instruments, prayer, church, and Christian community, even when they do not seem to be working. You keep going, mile by mile, until you've finally made it through.

The Paradox of God's Presence

Here is something paradoxical I have discovered. I have no fear now, facing cancer and chemotherapy. None. God is helping me fight through this with everything I have. Hundreds of people are praying for me, and I can feel their prayers like a tangible presence. The stars are bright, the compass is clear, the navigation is certain.

But during those years when I was searching for my purpose, when everything was objectively fine, that was when the clouds were thickest.

It seems backwards, does it not? Crisis brings clarity. When I was scared to death in a hotel in Saigon, I prayed with desperation and God felt close in the desperation. Now that I am facing cancer, I cling to God because there is nowhere else to turn. But when life was comfortable, when there was no urgent need, I drifted for years without realizing I lost sight of the stars.

David captured this in Psalm 22:1: "My God, my God, why have you forsaken me? Why are you so far from saving me, from the words of my groaning?" This is King David, the man after God's own heart. Yet even he experienced seasons when God seemed absent.

But notice how that psalm ends: "For he has not despised or abhorred the affliction of the afflicted, and he has not hidden his face from him, but has heard, when he cried to him" (Psalm 22:24). The feeling of abandonment was real, but it was not the reality. God had not actually hidden His face.

Tom Neary's Wake-Up Call

My friend Tom Neary had an experience in darkness that God used to drive him toward light. Tom had been diagnosed with a malignant tumor the size of a softball in his calf. It was the kind of diagnosis that stops your world cold. He was tough, intelligent, and successful, but nothing in his background had prepared him for the kind of fear that word, cancer, awakens.

During that season, Tom had what he later described as a vision or perhaps a dream of hell. He said it was more real than anything he had ever seen while awake. There were no flames, no cartoonish images of torment, only an overwhelming sense of separation from God. The loneliness, the despair, and the absence of love were unbearable. He woke up gasping, soaked in sweat, his heart pounding. His first words were, "If this is hell, I do not want any part of it."

That moment shook him to his core. It stripped away the layers of casual belief and the half-formed faith that had been comfortable enough when life was going well. Suddenly eternity was not an idea but a reality pressing in on him. The fear that followed was intense. He said there were days when he could hardly think about anything else, when the weight of that dream pressed on him like a physical burden.

But over time that fear did its holy work. It drove him to his knees, into Scripture, into prayer, and into a kind of surrender he had never known before. His desperation turned into faith, not because the fear disappeared, but because he discovered that only God could calm it. He began to realize that sometimes God allows the darkness not as punishment but as invitation into a deeper faith.

I love how Tom always ends the telling of this story. He would describe the terrible revelation of hell, his fear that followed, and then pause for a moment before saying in a quiet voice, "The darkness had a purpose. It made me desperate for light." Sometimes it takes the darkest places to make us reach for the brightest truth.

False Lights and True Navigation

During my various dark seasons, I encountered plenty of false lights, bits of advice and perspectives that sounded helpful at first but ultimately led nowhere.

People would say, "Just have more faith," as if faith were something you could summon through willpower or emotion, like flipping a switch. I would try to believe harder, to pray longer, to recite verses as if they were incantations, but it did not work. Faith itself is a gift from God which we receive through grace.

Other well-meaning friends would offer so-called pieces of advice like, "Everything happens for a reason." That statement may be true, but it is rarely helpful in the middle of darkness.

In the Catholic faith I converted to, much revolves around the sacraments, visible signs of invisible grace. They are beautiful, grounding, and holy reminders of God's presence in the physical world. Yet even the most sacred practices are not magic. It's possible to receive communion daily and still feel spiritually lost. You can go to confession regularly and still wrestle with the same doubts. The sacraments are means of receiving grace, not substitutes for the life-giving fullness that comes from a deep relationship with God.

The real question we can ask ourselves when feeling abandoned is this: Am I still seeking God? Romans 1 describes God's wrath as giving people over to their own choices. It is the chilling reality of God no longer protecting a person from the consequences of their rebellion. Here is the key: if you are worried that God has abandoned you, that worry itself is evidence that He has not. The truly abandoned do not care. They have stopped seeking altogether. The longing for His presence, even when met with silence, is the surest sign that His Spirit is still alive within you.

Sometimes the search itself is proof of faith. When you cannot see the stars, but you keep steering toward the last direction you knew was right, you are still navigating by truth.

Navigation Callout: Wreckers

Wrecking was a thriving business in the Florida Keys in the early 19th century. The term wrecking describes salvaging the cargo of ships that have run aground. Since the Florida Reef, especially near Key West, is a navigational challenge, the business of wrecking was profitable. At one point, wrecks were occurring at a rate of one per week. When vessels ran aground, there was a known process for the salvaging and claiming of the wreckage. Although not proven to be true, some legends describe haunting stories of wreckers who attempted to deliberately cause wrecks by using lanterns tied to donkeys or placed in a window to lure ships to dangerous run aground.

When the United States government got involved, they built light-houses to help reduce the number of wrecks. At first even these new lights caused wrecks as ship captains were confused about the lights that they were seeing and how that matched with their maps. During the Civil War, shipping through the Florida Straits declined and eventually more light-houses were built, better charts were developed and steam-powered vessels, which are less vulnerable to being pushed onto reefs , became more common and dramatically reduced the number of wrecks. By the end of the 19th century, wrecks on the Florida Reef were not common.

Although they likely were not legitimate threats in the Florida Keys, false lights are real threats in our spiritual journey. Choices and solutions that may ultimately lead to our destruction are not always obvious.Sometimes what looks like a guiding light may actually be leading you onto the rocks.

When the Clouds Finally Part

I cannot tell you when your clouds will lift. My own questions about purpose took years to resolve. The fear that shadowed me in Vietnam lasted through most of that entire tour. Some dark seasons stretch for days, others for decades. They are unpredictable and sometimes unbearably long.

But I can tell you this with certainty: Every spiritual darkness I have ever faced has eventually given way to light. Sometimes the change came so quietly that I did not recognize it until much later. There was no blinding sunrise, no dramatic revelation, only a gradual brightening, a slow return of warmth to a frozen heart. And then one day, almost imperceptibly, I looked up and realized the stars were visible again.

Psalm 23 captures this with an honesty that never loses its power. "Even though I walk through the valley of the shadow of death, I will fear no evil, for you are with me" (verse 4). Notice the wording. The Psalmist did not write "*If* I walk through the valley." Valleys are not detours in the life of faith; they are part of the journey.

Yet even more powerful is what comes next: "You are with me." Not I feel you with me, not I see you with me, but simply you are with me. It is a statement of fact, not emotion. When everything else is uncertain, the truth of God with us remains. God never stops being present in the darkness.

Practical Navigation for Dark Seasons

Through Vietnam's fear, through years of questioning my purpose, through various valleys, I've learned practical navigation techniques for when God seems absent:

Keep using the instruments. I went to church most Sundays in Vietnam, felt nothing, but kept going because I knew God was with me and I needed connection with Him. The practice of worship and gathering with other believers kept me tethered to my foundation.

Trust the map more than your feelings. The night in New York when I drove that young boy back to Young Life camp taught me this literally. The map was right even when I could barely see landmarks it showed. God's Word remains true even when you circumstances make feel like you're in a fog.

Remember that clouds are temporary. Even though difficult seasons may seem to stretch on without end, the clouds will lift. When I struggled with questions of doubt and purpose, I questioned this reality, but when God brought me through, I recognized that on the other side, the stars had never moved. God remained unchanged.

Let others navigate for you sometimes. We're not always as strong as we like to think. After my fall from the roof and during my current cancer journey, I've come to be grateful for the ways others come alongside and are used by God to keep me rooted in Him. Sometimes other people can see God at work in the situation more clearly than we can.

Recognize the paradox. God might feel closest in crisis and most distant when everything's fine. That doesn't mean He's moved—it means our perception changes based on our desperation. True North and Polaris are still there, unmoving.

If you're in the clouds right now, if God seems absent, if your prayers feel like they're going nowhere—keep navigating by instruments. Keep following the map even when you can barely see the landmarks. The clouds will lift. The stars are still there. God hasn't moved.

Coming Up Next...

The darkest storm—when cancer becomes your teacher and you discover God in the very place you thought He'd abandoned.

Chapter 13

The Darkest Storm

 I called out to the Lord, out of my distress, and he answered me; out of the belly of Sheol I cried, and you heard my voice.

— Jonah 2:2

As I write this, I am not looking back on the storm of my pancreatic cancer from a place of safety. I am still in it. The winds are real, the waters unpredictable, and each new day feels like another turn in a sea I do not fully understand.

When I journeyed through the diagnostic road, doctors checked all of the usual common sources for my symptoms. The dull ache didn't go away even though I changed my diet and tests for gallstones or a bile duct blockage came back negative. One test led to another, and the tone of my doctor's words shifted. His expressions grew more serious. The pauses lingered.

Then came the CT scan, the biopsy, and finally, the referral to oncology. Each appointment felt like walking farther into unfamiliar territory, the kind of terrain you study on a map but never expect to traverse yourself.

When the doctor said the word "malignant," it seemed to hang in the air like a sound that would not dissipate. Tami was sitting beside me, her hand in mine. In over sixty years of marriage, we have faced deployments, injuries, career transitions, and countless ordinary storms. But this was different. This was not just another challenge to overcome. It was an entirely new map.

We left the office in silence. I remember noticing how ordinary the world still looked, people walking by the windows, cars moving through traffic, sunlight reflecting off windshields. Everything appeared normal, but nothing was normal anymore. A single word had redrawn the horizon.

The recommended Whipple procedure would remove the head of my pancreas, along with part of my stomach, my duodenum, and my gallbladder. The surgeon was confident yet honest. "We will know more once we are in there," he said. It was the kind of phrase meant to prepare you for uncertainty, but there is no real preparation for that kind of unknown.

When the day of surgery arrived, I remember being wheeled into the bright, sterile lights of the operating room. Machines hummed quietly. Nurses spoke with calm professionalism. I thought of the maps I used to draw in my early years with the Air Force: lines, contours, elevations, all so precise. Now I was the one being charted, my body the landscape to be explored and repaired.

They told me afterward that the surgery lasted over eleven hours. They found cancer cells in nearby lymph nodes, meaning the cancer had already spread. Their words were clinical, but the weight of them was immense.

What we knew at that moment was enough. I was entering the darkest part of my journey, the one that would test not just my strength, but everything I had ever believed about God, life, and trust. This was not theoretical faith anymore. This was the kind that either holds when everything else falls away, or it does not hold at all.

And yet, even here, as I'm in the middle of this uncharted sea, I have found that God is still the same navigator He has always been. The instruments still work. The compass still points North. The stars are still above the clouds, even when I cannot see them. That part is normal even though nothing else is.

When You Must Face Your Deepest Fears

Polar night is the phenomenon that occurs in the north and south poles when the sun doesn't rise for over twenty-four hours. Places like the far polar regions experience this lack of light for a couple of months each year. Living without daylight for such a prolonged period is proven to have a variety of effects on humans ranging from insomnia to Seasonal Affective Disorder (SAD), to reduced creativity and less ability to concentrate.

A cancer diagnosis feels like living in the polar night. I am on a continuous and inescapable journey into an unrevealed landscape. Even the landscape I've previously known feels unfamiliar and my landmarks have disappeared. Navigation tools I've relied on for decades suddenly seem inadequate. The habits and prayers that once brought comfort feel muted. Even hopes for better days ahead grow dim under the weight of uncertainty.

Every person carries fundamental fears that lie beneath everyday anxieties. For many of us who have lived into our eighties, it is not death itself that we fear most. It is the journey toward it. It is the possibility of losing independence. It is the dread of becoming a burden on our families. It is the anticipation of pain. It is the slow reduction of who we have been until we hardly recognize ourselves.

Cancer brings all of those fears to the surface at once. One day I was planning home repairs, family visits, and small projects. The next day I was studying survival rates, learning medical terminology, and signing forms for procedures I'd never heard of before. Someone has taken my map and turned it upside down.

The night before surgery, I could not sleep. I stared at the ceiling in the hospital's pre-surgical ward and listened to the hum of machines. I thought about our eight grandchildren. I thought about the Christmas book I still wanted to write for the family, the stories and prayers I wanted to put into their hands. I thought about the conversations not yet had and the wisdom not yet shared.

But mostly, I thought about God. Where was He in this? I had navigated by His presence for decades, but lying there under the fluorescent lights, I felt very alone. The stars were not just hidden behind clouds. They seemed to have been extinguished entirely.

And yet, even in that darkness, a small, steady truth kept surfacing in my mind. It was not an emotional comfort or a warm feeling. I simply remembered that God had not moved. Even though I could not see Him, He had not left. In the Great Dark of my own polar night, that was the only thing I could hold on to.

The Valley Where All Light Fails

In the last chapter, I wrote about Psalm 23 and its promise that even in the valley of the shadow of death, God remains present. Prior to cancer, the valley was still a metaphor to me. Career setbacks, spiritual droughts, and even the fall from the roof were valleys of a kind, but they were not yet the true shadow of death.

When my favorite uncle, who was like a second father to me, was dying of melanoma, I read Psalm 23 at his hospital bedside. Tami and I had been married just a year, and he had attended our wedding. Not long after, he was facing his final storm.

He had developed a mole on the bottom of his foot. They operated and removed it, but the cancer had already spread. My father drove him to Mayo Clinic, where the doctors did all they could, but it was too late. His physician, Dr. Reese, who knew I was considering medical school, handed me a book called The Doctors Mayo, a history of the clinic. I still have it.

At that point in life my understanding of God was new. I had just converted to Catholicism and had been baptized, but my relationship with God had not deepened. But I remember standing by that bedside, reading Psalm 23 as a goodbye. It felt awkward, uncertain, even risky to read aloud, but it also felt necessary. Somehow I knew those words needed to be spoken. That moment became a core memory of a time that God's presence was real and very much needed.

Now, decades later, with cancer pressing in on my own life, that psalm has taken on a new and raw reality. What had once been words of comfort spoken over another has become a lifeline I cling to myself.

My life has had challenges and God has even brought me to situations where I needed to rely on Him. I see that those lessons were preparing me for this greater storm of cancer because let me tell you, cancer is different. It takes the metaphors described in Psalm 23 and makes them literal. The shadow of death is not poetic language anymore; it is the actual shadow cast by mortality moving closer than ever before.

I think about Captain William Bligh's navigation miracle after the mutiny on the Bounty in 1789. He and eighteen loyal crewmen were sent off in a twenty-three-foot open boat with no charts, minimal supplies, and navigation tools of only a compass, quadrant, and a pocket watch. For forty-seven days they faced storms, starvation, and hostile islands until they reached the nearest European settlement. Bligh was an excellent navigator, having worked with and been praised by Captain James Cook, yet without proper tools and supplies his navigation skills were put to the test.

That is what living with cancer feels like. Even though previously it was possible to live under an illusion of having control and knowing what to expect out of life, a diagnosis like cancer changes the circumstances entirely. I feel like Bligh, navigating without proper charts, with limited resources, through hostile waters, all while never being certain whether I'm moving toward healing or deeper into the storm.

Jesus in His Own Darkest Hour

Undergoing chemotherapy gave me a new perspective on the Gospel accounts of Jesus in Gethsemane. When Jesus, the Son of God, faced His own appointment with suffering, what did He do? He prayed for it to be removed. "My Father, if it be possible, let this cup pass from me" (Matthew 26:39).

That prayer has become one of the most comforting in all of Scripture for me. Jesus knew the plan. He understood the necessity of the cross. He was one with the Father. Yet in the garden, He still asked for another way. That honesty has sustained me and brought me courage. If Jesus Himself could pray for the suffering to pass, then surely my own prayers for healing, my own struggle to accept this path, are not faithless. They are deeply human.

During one particularly difficult chemotherapy session, when the drugs were making me sick and the neuropathy was setting in, I found myself praying a shorter version of that same prayer. "I don't understand this, but I trust You." That simple prayer came from a deep place of honest struggle. It wasn't eloquent but revealed my acknowledgement to and submission to God's will.

Many people know of John Newton and his story. He was the former slave trader who became a minister and wrote "Amazing Grace." Newton's life is fascinating and he experienced dramatic conversion from a slave trader to a vocal abolitionist. We've discussed the challenges of navigating through storms extensively in this book and it was in a storm at sea that Newton became a Christian. He survived that storm and gradually his life turned around completely.

While "Amazing Grace" is his most well-known song, Newton wrote 280 hymns, many which he wrote to accompany his sermons. The first stanza of his hymn, "I Will Trust and Not be Afraid" is so applicable to the trials of life, and especially significant for me in this storm of cancer that I'm currently experiencing.

> *Begone, unbelief, my Savior is near*
> *And for my relief will surely appear.*
> *By prayer let me wrestle, and He will perform;*
> *With Christ in the vessel, I smile at the storm.*

Walking with God through this storm of cancer is the reason I can have hope and smile through the uncertainty.

Finding God in the Heart of the Storm

While I understand God is with me through every step of my journey, the reality of His presence is not always tangible. Initially, I expected to find God in miraculous healing. My actual experience has been that He reveals Himself in places I haven't expected. I've found Him in the oncology nurse who knows exactly when to offer encouragement and when to simply be silent. I expected flashes of revelation or dramatic spiritual experiences. Instead, I have found Him in Tami's endless patience as she drives me to another appointment, in the small improvements in my blood work, and in the simple mercy of being able to eat a meal without nausea.

There's another hymn writer's story that I think of often. Horatio Spafford wrote the hymn "It Is Well With My Soul" in 1873. His story has always moved me, but never more than now. He lost most of his real estate investment in the Chicago Fire and his four daughters when their ship sank while crossing the Atlantic. As he sailed to meet his grieving wife after their daughters had died at sea, he wrote this hymn as his boat passed over the place where his girls had drowned. There, he wrote the words that have comforted millions:

> *When peace like a river attendeth my way,*
> *When sorrows like sea billows roll,*
> *Whatever my lot, Thou hast taught me to say,*
> *It is well, it is well with my soul.*

Years later, Spafford suffered loss when his young son succumbed to scarlet fever. Yet these tragedies pushed Spafford and his wife closer to God than before. He praised God not because God prevented hard times, but because He found God in the exact middle of the hard times. That is what I am discovering too. God is not only the rescuer who stills the storm; He is also the companion who sits with us in the boat when the waves are high.

The Unexpected Lights in the Darkness

We've all heard stories of situations where good times have come out of terrible circumstances. After natural disasters, communities are often strengthened because of the way neighbors help each other. In October 2012, Hurricane Sandy moved up the eastern coast and brought devastation along with it. People lost power and didn't have heat while sand and mud clogged the streets. In the aftermath, volunteers arrived and set up tents to distribute water and food, helped clean up, and gave away gift cards so people could rebuild their lives. The disaster was terrible, but because of the storm people experienced the beauty of kindness and relationships that wouldn't have been built otherwise.

Cancer has brought similar unexpected grace into my own darkness. On a daily basis I don't see sweeping miracles or experience dramatic victories, but I have been shown small kindnesses and grown in unexpected ways that have kept me moving forward even when these days feel long.

It's funny how when life brings mortality upfront and personal, suddenly there is clarity about what matters in life and what really does not. Old grudges I've carried have faded and minor irritations that I might mull over for days no longer matter. As the noise of life has quieted, what remains is love for God, for family, and for friends. I don't know what the future will bring, but I do have a sense that time feels shorter which makes each day more precious and my priorities have become startlingly clear. Most of what once troubled me is easier to let go and my biggest desire is to focus on the things that endure like loving well and leaving behind something that reflects that love.

Tami is with me through all of this and as we walk this journey together we have a deeper intimacy than ever before in our nearly sixty years of marriage. No marriage conference or retreat would have had the same kind of effect as cancer has. Love has taken on a deep texture as she helps me at three in the morning, drives me to another appointment without complaint, and sits quietly beside me through hours of chemotherapy. It becomes less about words and more about presence. We are learning how marriage in suffering becomes a form of worship, an embodied experience of patience and grace.

For so many years, I took simple things for granted. I trusted that my body would move and function properly and I didn't think much about the freedom there is in independence. Now, I am grateful for many small things. I celebrate the days without nausea and delight when my taste for food returns after weeks of blandness. When I feel strong enough to walk to the mailbox and back, it's a small mercy worthy of celebrating. Moments of reprieve feel like sunlight breaking through clouds and for those I am completely grateful because life is not easy, and I notice even the small blessings.

This slowed down and intentionally grateful lifestyle is common amongst the connections I've made at the cancer treatment center which has become a kind of fellowship hall for the wounded. In the waiting rooms, I see faces from every background, each marked by a mix of fear, courage, and quiet endurance. We rarely talk about diagnoses. We talk about grandchildren, hobbies, or good recipes. We laugh when we can. A nod or smile from another patient sometimes carries more encouragement than any sermon. In those moments, I sense the body of Christ in its truest form—ordinary people carrying one another through the storm.

These are the unexpected lights I've found in my cancer journey. They do not erase the darkness, but they make it navigable.

Navigation Callout: The Bermuda Triangle's Simple Truth

The Bermuda Triangle—that supposedly deadly stretch of ocean between Florida, Bermuda, and Puerto Rico—has captured imaginations for decades. Conspiracy theories abound speculating over the reasons for mysterious disappearances in that area. Perhaps Christopher Columbus' notes that documented odd compass readings and unusual lights in the sky began the special attention on the "Bermuda Triangle." But reputable organizations including reinsurer Lloyd's of London, the United States Coast Guard, and the National Oceanic and Atmospheric Administration (NOAA) have analyzed data of disappearances reported in this area and determined that these occurrences are not higher than in any other heavily traveled area of the ocean.

Our minds love a good mystery and the hype around the Bermuda Triangle has been a source that plays into our great fears. Sometimes our deepest fears are scarier in our imagination than in reality. God is present even in our "Bermuda Triangles."

Reflection and Application

As I continue through chemotherapy, I've found it helpful to keep a notebook and pen close to chart my passages through dark waters. Consider doing this for your own storms by pausing to consider your path before, during, and after a storm.

Before the Storm:

- What was life like before this trial began?
- What did you take for granted?
- What storms did you fear might come?

In the Storm's Center:

- Where have you unexpectedly found light?
- What resources are keeping you afloat?
- What are you learning that calm seas never could have taught?

After the Storm (for past trials):

- How did the trial change your navigation skills?
- What new instruments did you gain?
- How has it equipped you to guide others?

Still in the Storm

As I write these words, my journey through the storm of cancer has not passed. Some days are better than others yet the prognosis remains uncertain. Even though I've navigated countless storms through the course of my life, I still have much to learn about living, navigating through life, when I can't see the path ahead.

The darkness is real, and the waters can feel bottomless, but even here God is present. In fact, I have discovered that He is most visible here, as everything else disappears. He certainly won't abandon me now simply because the weather has turned severe.

Coming Up Next...

Emerging from the storm—discovering that God was there all along, learning to trust the instruments when the stars return, and finding your new normal with Romans 12:12 as your guide.

Chapter 14

Emerging from the Storm

 Be joyful in hope, patient in affliction, faithful in prayer.

— Romans 12:12 NIV

This verse has become my theme as I navigate through this cancer journey I am on. Tami may have written it on a card for me, or perhaps I have simply memorized it by repetition, tracing the words until they became part of my heartbeat. Either way, it has become my three-point compass: joy for perspective, patience for endurance, prayer for connection.

The Slow Dawn of Understanding

After my Whipple surgery and the news that the cancer had spread to my lymph nodes, I expected one of two things. Either a miraculous recovery that would astonish my doctors, or a steady decline that would prepare my family for what was coming. What I received instead was something in between, a slow and uneven journey through the long middle of chemotherapy. There were weeks when I felt almost normal, followed by days when I could not move without exhaustion. Hope and discouragement traded places so often that I stopped trying to predict which one would arrive next.

God continues to show His nearness in tangible ways. The oncology nurse practitioner who seemed to know when to speak and when to sit in silence shows me God's care. Friends from church, or neighbors who arrive unannounced with a prayer, or a meal, or a word that fit perfectly to the need of that day have been another sign. Another faithful friend brings us lunch at every chemotherapy appointment. His faithfulness serves to break up a long day and brings joy to our hearts. Yet another great spiritual gift is the Eucharistic Minister, Joe, who comes to our house every Sunday with Holy Communion. What a gift from God as I work through this trial in my life. And then, of course, there is Tami's steady presence through every appointment, every uncertain report, every difficult night. She is a living embodiment of divine love.

When God didn't immediately and miraculously heal me and my body didn't decline rapidly, I knew God had a longer-term plan for using this sickness. Somehow I made it to this point in life without understanding that He is near, even in the ordinary. He doesn't hide and I can see this through the kindness of others and His love that endures even when everything else feels fragile.

Job's Unexpected Restoration

Let's take a look into the life of Job. His story carries new weight for me now. After all his suffering, all his questions, and all the misguided counsel from his friends, God finally speaks to him out of the whirl-wind. What strikes me most is what God does not say. He does not offer explanations or apologies for Job's suffering. He does not justify Himself or fill in the gaps of Job's understanding. Instead, He asks His own question: "Where were you when I laid the foundation of the earth?" (Job 38:4).

Then there are four chapters where God unfolds a vision of creation's vastness. He speaks of the boundaries of the sea, the store-houses of snow, the wildness of lions and mountain goats, the mysteries of light and darkness. God uses these reminders of His character to demonstrate to Job a message that, "I am God and you are not. I see what you cannot see. I understand what you cannot understand." Those words should feel cold and distant, yet they do not. Somehow, in God's thunderous speech, Job does not feel smaller in a humiliating way, but smaller in a holy way. The scale of divine wisdom humbles him into peace.

Job's response captures the heart of transformation: "I had heard of you by the hearing of the ear, but now my eye sees you" (Job 42:5).

Seeing is personal. I echo those words of Job's, because I see God in new ways. I have heard about God's faithfulness my entire life. I have read about it, talked about it, and shared it with others. I've never doubted God's faithfulness, but now, in the crucible of this disease, I see it constantly in my life. All of my questions aren't answered the way I would like and I still battle moments of confusion and fear, but a deeper trust in God outweighs the unknowns.

When the book of Job ends, his restoration is often summarized in material terms: his health returns, his family grows again, and his wealth is doubled. But that is not the real restoration. The true restoration is internal. Job's spiritual sight is restored. His heart learns to see God as He truly is. That is why Job's final confession rings with such confidence: "I know that you can do all things, and that no purpose of yours can be thwarted" (Job 42:2).

That is what I now call navigation confidence. When you no longer see where you are going, you can still rest in knowing who is steering the vessel. Perhaps that is the deepest kind of faith: not sight restored in the way we expect, but sight redefined by trust.

Learning to Read the Storm Patterns

Through months of chemotherapy, I have become something of a storm expert. Not in avoiding storms, but in learning how to navigate through them. Storms have their own logic, their own patterns. Hurricanes are a perfect example of this. As a hurricane builds it gathers strength and forms into the familiar swirling image with the eye at the center. When a hurricane makes landfall, it starts with raindrops and breezy wind which become stronger. These are the rainbands. Then the storm progresses into the driving rain and damaging sustained winds which is the eyewall. This most destructive part arrives right ahead of the eye, the calm center of the storm when the winds die down and the sun may even appear. That's not the end of the storm though because the other side of the eyewall arrives next, bringing more damaging wind and rain until the storm breaks apart into the outer rainbands.

I often feel like I'm in this hurricane structure. There are the physical cycles, the rhythm of treatment and recovery. Day one may feel manageable, while days two and three bring fatigue, weakness, and discouragement. Then comes a gradual lightening, a stretch of steadier waters before the next round begins. The pattern is not always predictable, but it is learnable. When I stopped fighting the rhythm and began planning for it, I found that peace was possible even in repetition. Understanding and being able to predict suffering is a small grace.

There are also emotional weather systems that move through the heart. They arrive suddenly, without warning. I regularly experience a wave of sadness, a surge of fear, or a flash of unexpected joy. I used to think these fluctuations meant my faith was weak, but now I understand they are simply part of the atmosphere of endurance. Real faith does not erase emotion; it steadies you enough to feel it without being carried away. You do not outrun the storm; you pass through it, trusting the One who commands the wind.

Then there are the patterns of divine timing. Help seems to arrive precisely when it is needed. Never early, because that would cancel the lesson of trust, and never late, because God's timing is perfect. A handwritten note appears on the day discouragement threatens to take over. A phone call comes just when the isolation feels heavy. A good test result arrives at the exact moment hope was slipping away. These are not coincidences. They are coordinates on the spiritual map, markers of God's presence.

The Storm That Jesus Rebuked

Do you remember the storm that Jesus calmed? This experience out on the Sea of Galilee tested even the instincts of Jesus' disciples who were experienced fishermen. Jesus and His followers were crossing the Sea of Galilee when a violent wind rose up, sending waves crashing into their boat. These men who had weathered storms before, were terrified. They cried out, "Teacher, do you not care that we are perishing?" (Mark 4:38).

Jesus woke, rebuked the wind, and said to the waves, "Peace, be still." The storm fell silent. Then He turned to His disciples and asked, "Why are you so afraid? Have you still no faith?" (Mark 4:40).

For years, I read those questions as a rebuke, as if Jesus were disappointed in their fear. Now, from the middle of my own storm, I hear it differently. It is not a scolding question but a tender invitation. The disciples mistook His rest for indifference, but His peace was the lesson. He was asleep because He trusted completely in the Father's care. His stillness in the storm was not neglect; it was divine confidence.

My cancer storm has not been calmed with a single word. The waves are still high, and the wind still howls. Yet I am beginning to understand what Jesus was teaching that day. The goal is not the disappearance of the storm, but the discovery of who is in the boat. His presence is the true peace.

Storms reveal the difference between belief and trust. Belief knows the truth in theory; trust lives it when the waters rise. I am learning that the truest kind of faith is not proven when the sea is calm but when the boat rocks and you choose, again and again, to stay near the One who controls the storms.

Romans 12:12: A New Navigation System

"Be joyful in hope, patient in affliction, faithful in prayer" (NIV).

As I said at the beginning of this chapter, this verse has become my three-point navigation system through cancer:

Joyful in hope—not joyful about cancer, but joyful in the hope that transcends it. Hope that God is working even in this. Hope that nothing is wasted in God's economy. Hope that the story isn't over. This joy isn't giddy happiness; it's a deep-seated confidence that God is still good, still sovereign, still working. And my hope is that whatever comes of this journey I am on, that the result would glorify God.

Patient in affliction—patience here isn't passive waiting but active endurance. It's showing up for another round of chemotherapy. It's managing the side effects without despair. It's giving the treatment time to work, giving my body time to fight, and believing God's timing is perfect. It's understanding that some journeys can't be rushed.

Faithful in prayer—not perfect in prayer, not eloquent in prayer, but faithful. Showing up. Keeping the conversation going. Some days this looks like desperate pleading. Other days it's simple gratitude. Sometimes it's wordless groaning. But always it's connection, always it's turning toward God rather than away.

The Unexpected Competence

In this long journey through cancer. I have become more competent at reading the spiritual maps of my life. I am learning to navigate by faith rather than by sight, to trust even when visibility is poor. The very storm that once threatened to undo my faith has, paradoxically, made it stronger.

It reminds me of learning to navigate in dense fog. When you first enter fog, the disorientation is complete. You slow down, and move cautiously even though your heart pounds with certainty that collision is imminent. Every sound seems amplified, every moment stretched thin by the unknown. Yet as you move down the road, something remarkable happens. You start to read the subtle cues: the faint reflection of light on water, the glimpses of the lines on the road, and in familiarity an instinct of the road allows you to keep on moving.

That is what faith in suffering does. It trains you to move through spiritual fog. I am reading Scripture differently now. Verses about endurance, hope, and trust that once felt abstract speak deeply to my specific terrain. Paul's thorn in the flesh no longer reads like distant theology but like a brother's confession. Job's questions feel like ones I've asked myself. The psalmists' cries from the depths have become the language of my own prayers.

It's in this suffering that my prayers have changed. My heart cries out with an outpouring that I sometimes don't even recognize. God is my close companion and many times I'm content to sit quietly in His presence without a focus on trying to convince Him to act in the way I think is best. In prayer I've shifted from trying to change God's mind to letting Him change mine. I understand that He knows the route, even when I do not.

Suffering has made me a better navigator. I trust the compass more than the horizon.

The Rainbow Principle

After the Old Testament flood, God gave Noah a sign of promise. "I have set my bow in the cloud, and it shall be a sign of the covenant between me and the earth" (Genesis 9:13). Rainbows don't appear in clear skies. They're visible and most brilliant in the lingering mist, when sunlight and elements of the storm mingle together. The beauty of the rainbow requires both—the remnant of rain and the returning light.

That image has become precious to me. I am living in what I call the rainbow moment. My storm of cancer has not fully ended, but there are moments when light breaks through. Every good test result is a kind of rainbow, a glimmer of grace cutting through uncertainty. Every day when I am strong enough to write or to walk outside is another rainbow. Every quiet meal with Tami, every game we play, every shared laugh with family, every prayer that ends with peace instead of fear is another stripe of color across the gray sky.

There is a kind of joy that can only be found when the storm and sunlight meet. It is the joy of knowing that God's covenant still holds, that His presence remains constant, and that the light of His faithfulness will always find a way through the clouds.

Navigation Callout: GPS Selective Availability

From 1990 to 2000, the U.S. military intentionally degraded civilian GPS signals through a feature called Selective Availability. Civilian GPS units could only pinpoint location within about 100 meters, close enough to be useful, but not precise. Then, President Clinton ordered this feature to be turned off which happened at midnight on May 1, 2000. Overnight, civilian GPS accuracy improved to within 20 meters. Millions of GPS users worldwide suddenly found their navigation five times more precise.

Sometimes God improves our spiritual accuracy just as suddenly. He can reveal Himself in fresh ways that deepen our understanding of Him instantly. Throughout most of my life I navigated with degraded signals, seeing dimly, understanding partially until suddenly God improved the precision of my understanding of Him. I didn't become a better navigator, but God removed whatever was limiting my spiritual GPS.

For months after my cancer diagnosis, I navigated with degraded signals. I could see God was there, somewhere in that 100-meter radius, but I couldn't pinpoint His presence precisely. I knew He was working, but I couldn't see how. At some point in that journey, my ability to detect God sharpened. The same God who'd been there all along became clearer, more precise, more locatable.

Paul wrote about this in his first letter to the Corinthian church. He wrote, "For now we see in a mirror dimly, but then face to face. Now I know in part; then I shall know fully, even as I have been fully known" (1 Corinthians 13:12). I am looking forward to the time when my spiritual understanding of God will be face to face.

What I Know Now

I know that God's presence is not measured by my ability to feel it. During the first days after the diagnosis, when fear drowned out every prayer and the future felt like a blank map, He was no less present than He is now. The silence did not mean God was absent and looking back, I can trace His fingerprints across every phase of this journey.

Smooth sailing never trained anyone to steer by faith. A good navigator becomes good by experiencing the challenges of staying on course in the middle of the storms. We've looked at several skilled navigators in this book, and they undoubtedly would not have had such success in reaching their destinations if they had not learned what to do in the pressure of storms. It is in the chaos of wind and waves that we learn to trust in what we know to be true. I am a better spiritual navigator because of cancer, not in spite of it.

Although this is not a pleasant reality, we recognize that God's goal for us is not to necessarily take us out of the storm, but to walk with us and reveal more of Himself as we navigate through. Often His purposes are to teach us how to move through, one prayer at a time, one breath at a time, one act of trust at a time. Storms are not God's interruptions to the journey but classrooms designed by the Master Navigator. They shape us into the kind of person who can help others through their own storms.

Your Storm Navigation

If you're in a storm right now, whether it's cancer, loss of a loved one, failure, or any other trial, know this: the storm doesn't last forever, but more importantly, God is in it with you. Maybe you feel like your GPS has Selective Availability enabled, but the degraded signals you're navigating with now won't always be degraded. One day, maybe gradually, maybe suddenly, the precision will improve. You'll look back and see that God was there working in ways you couldn't perceive.

Until then, navigate by whatever light you have. Use Romans 12:12 as your compass: Stay joyful in hope, patient in affliction, faithful in prayer. Learn to understand the storm patterns. Watch for rainbows. Trust that the Navigator knows where you're going even when you don't.

The storm is real. But so is the God who calms the winds and waves with a single word and who brings beauty from chaos.

Keep sailing. Keep trusting. Keep watching for the rainbow.

Coming Up Next...

Finding North in family—how God uses those closest to us as navigation aids, and discovering that sometimes our greatest purpose is found in the legacy we're building through ordinary faithfulness.

Chapter 15

Finding North in Family

 Grandchildren are the crown of the aged, and the glory of children is their fathers.

— Proverbs 17:6

We have already explored how relationships can redirect our compass. How Tami helped me find my bearings when I was drifting in college. How mentors appeared at just the right moments in my career. How our son and daughter's Young Life experience reshaped the direction of our entire family. But family itself deserves its own place in the story.

Family is not like other relationships. It is not just another navigation aid along the way. Family is the anchor. It holds you steady when the winds are strong, when you have lost sight of the shore, when you are too weary to steer.

I did not recognize that truth immediately. Few people do. It took me years, maybe decades, to understand it fully. For a long time, I believed my purpose was tied to achievement. I thought it was about what I could contribute through my work, my service, my ministry. Those things mattered, of course, but they were never the center of the map.

The revelation came slowly, as our children began raising families of their own. Somewhere in the middle of watching them parent, I realized that my true purpose was not just to have a family, but to help nurture a living faith that could continue long after I am gone. To help build a spiritual foundation strong enough to support not just my children but their children, and theirs after them.

When Your Children Become Your Teachers

I have already told the story of our son's Young Life weekend, how he came home changed. We had raised him in church, prayed together, and taught him what we could about faith. But after that retreat, he came back different. He had met Christ personally. The faith that had been ours became his.

What I did not expect was how much his transformation would change Tami and me. We had assumed our role was to teach our children about faith. Instead, God used our son and daughter to teach us. Their enthusiasm, their joy, and their personal relationship with Christ revealed how traditional and routine my own faith had become.

Both of our children live out their faith in their daily lives. Our daughter is a high school teacher in Virginia and has brought her faithfulness to the classroom. Her husband Tom is also a teacher and does the same for his students. Our son spent thirteen years on Young Life staff, walking alongside high school students who were asking the same questions he once had.

It is humbling when your child becomes your teacher. But I've seen how this can be God's design. In our case He let the next generation find their own route to Him, and in doing so, they led us, their parents, into deeper waters. This back and forth encouragement is one of the ways He keeps faith alive and growing from one generation to the next.

The Generational View

When you are young, your navigation is self-oriented. You think mostly about your own direction and what God might be calling you to do. In midlife, your focus shifts. You start navigating for your family, making choices that will protect and guide them. But something changes again when you become a grandparent. The horizon widens. You begin to see your life not as a single voyage but as part of a much longer journey.

We have eight grandchildren now, and recently, a great-grandchild. Watching them grow, seeing our children raise families of their own, has given me a new sense of purpose. I am no longer just navigating my own course. I am helping to leave behind a map that they can follow when I am gone.

Sometimes I watch them at family gatherings and catch glimpses of God's faithfulness in the smallest things. The way the grandchildren bow their heads before a meal. The sound of our children talking about faith as naturally as they talk about work or daily life. It is clear evidence that something we prayed for long ago is still unfolding.

I once believed my purpose was to navigate well. Now I see that it was also to leave a path behind. Something my family could walk when they face their own storms.

Family, I have learned, is more than what keeps you steady. It is what makes the journey worth taking in the first place.

Branch One: Our Daughter's Two (The Adopted Line)

Our daughter's faith story has never followed the dramatic arc of sudden conversion or crisis. It has been a steady unfolding, like dawn breaking slowly across the horizon. She remained anchored in the Catholic Church from childhood, deepening her faith gradually, almost quietly, over the years.

After college, she began teaching high school history and government, bringing faith into her classroom not through overt preaching but through the way she treated her students with patience, fairness, and kindness. Her classroom often felt more like a mentorship than a lecture hall.

During those years, she joined a traveling singing group called The Continental Singers. Somewhere between the long bus rides and the late-night concerts, Tom pursued her. He was drawn to her from the start, and from what she tells, he was persistent. He even showed up at her concerts when she was on the road, finding excuses to be near her.

Tom came from a strong Protestant background. His brother is a Methodist minister, and his parents lived their faith with dedicated consistency. When he and our daughter married, they brought two different expressions of Christian faith together, and somehow the result was richer. They have built a deeply rooted Catholic life at Nativity Catholic Church in Burke, Virginia, where Tom now teaches math and robotics to grade schoolers. He is a demonstration of how faith and reason can coexist in one person's vocation.

Years ago, they adopted two boys from Russia. They came as tiny, one-year-olds who brought with them just the faintest memories of their beginnings. Noah was first, and then three years later Joshua joined their family. These were both very difficult processes with long trips to Russia, spending weeks in the country both times. Raising adopted children has brought both joy and heartache, a mixture that only parents who have lived it can understand. Watching those two boys grow into such different young men has been one of the clearest lessons I have ever seen in God's mysterious providence.

Noah has flourished. He is bright, disciplined, and deeply grounded. Now serving in the Navy, he has been selected for the nuclear program, an honor reserved for the most capable and determined. His training has already taken him to Charleston, South Carolina, and will soon bring him to Groton, Connecticut, for submarine school. When I think of Noah, I see a young man who has taken the faith of his parents and made it his own. He reminds me that God calls people into all kinds of vocations, sometimes even into the depths of the sea.

Joshua has had a harder path. He is a kind young man, quick to help with chores around the house or in the yard, and he has a smile that can light up a room. But he carries wounds that may trace back to his earliest days before adoption, in those first fragile months that shape so much of who we become. His struggles have taken him into a rehabilitation program where he is still searching for his footing. His journey weighs heavily on our hearts, yet it has also deepened our prayers. We trust that God has not lost sight of him.

There are days when the waiting for God to move feels endless, but love is patient, and faith endures. We hold fast to the hope that the family anchor, the web of love and prayer that surrounds him, will hold until he finds his way home.

This too is legacy.

Legacy is not just the graduations, the weddings, or the birth announcements. It is also the persistent prayers for the one who wanders, the faith to believe when there is no evidence, and the determination to never stop loving. Joshua's story is still being written, and we will keep turning the pages until grace finishes what it started.

Branch Two: Our Son's Six (The Grove City, PA Line)

Tami and I often talk about how God has shaped our son's family. There is no other way to explain it. What we see in them now, their faith, their unity, and their joy, is the fruit of many years of obedience and daily choices. All six of their children have been deeply influenced by faith, by Grove City College in western Pennsylvania, and by a strong church community that has surrounded them since they were small. Five of our grandchildren have already attended Grove City, and the youngest is still in high school, preparing for his turn.

We have told parts of Trent's story before, how his faith grew through years of Young Life leadership and a steady love for the Lord. But that story has stretched across nearly three decades of marriage now. It has been refined by time, by work, and by the joys and trials of raising a large family.

Wendy's story intertwines beautifully with his. She was born and raised in Pennsylvania in a family that lived out their Christian faith in word and deed. Her parents, Peggy and Bill, modeled a life centered on Jesus. Peggy continues to lead worship at their church, and Bill, one of the most natural evangelists I ever met, used his passion for fly fishing as a doorway to sharing the gospel. He truly was a fisher of men, and now he rests with the Lord. Wendy's sisters, Carrie and Maurie, both serve faithfully as well. One is married to a pastor in Vancouver, British Columbia, and the other to a doctor who works with Native American communities in Arizona.

About thirty years ago, Wendy moved to Maryland. She was looking for someone to run with, both literally and spiritually. A cousin suggested she connect with the local Young Life leader. That leader turned out to be Trent. They started running together, first as friends, then as something more, and before long they were running the race of life side by side. Wendy is an athlete through and through. Together, she and Trent have completed both the Marine Corps and Boston Marathons.

Today, their lives are centered around service. Trent is a real estate agent and serves as an elder in their church, and Wendy now works there full time. Every Friday morning, they open their home for a pancake breakfast. Dozens of high school students crowd into their kitchen to eat, talk, and hear about Jesus before school starts. It is messy, loud, and full of life, the kind of ministry Jesus would have loved.

Seeing how our son and daughter-in-law have built their lives around faith has deepened my own. Their consistency, their compassion, and their willingness to make room for others have been a living sermon to me.

The Next Generation

Madeline

Our oldest grandchild, Madeline, recently made us great-grandparents. She and her husband, Zach, welcomed their first child, a beautiful little girl named Hadley. Madeline works for Young Life, serving high school and college students and helping them encounter Christ for themselves. Zach, who also loves the Lord, works at Grove City College and comes from a wonderful Christian family. Watching them begin this new chapter fills me with gratitude. There is something indescribably moving about seeing your faith carried forward into yet another generation.

Brett

Madeline's brother Brett also graduated from Grove City. His testimony continues to inspire me. For years, sports were his identity. When injuries and disappointments threatened that identity, he discovered what it meant to find worth in Christ instead of performance. His story reminds me that failure can be one of God's most effective teachers. Brett now mentors others, helping them navigate that same shift from self-reliance to faith.

Rachel

Rachel, another Grove City graduate, now teaches art at a private K–12 school. Her commute is long, but she never complains. She brings faith and creativity together in her teaching, using beauty as a doorway to truth. She also serves actively in her church and with Young Life, giving students a glimpse of God's creativity through her own.

Tyler

Tyler shares his mother's athleticism and his father's energy. He recently got engaged to Morgan, a wonderful young woman from a strong Christian family. Their wedding is planned for August 2026. Tyler has a contagious joy that draws people in. His faith shines naturally, through his presence. You simply feel better when he is around.

Alex

Alex is studying engineering at Grove City. He is quieter than his siblings, but thoughtful and wise beyond his years. He notices what others miss and steps in without being asked. There is a quiet strength in him, the kind that often marks great leaders later in life. His faith is steady and unpretentious, the kind that lasts.

Chase

Our youngest grandson, Chase, is still in high school but already dreaming big. He has joined the Civil Air Patrol and started flight lessons. He hopes to one day fly jets for the Air Force. His room is full of model airplanes and flight manuals, but beneath all that ambition is a genuine love for God. He prays before takeoff, even in the simulator. I suspect his flight path will be just as guided by faith as his siblings' journeys have been.

A Living Legacy

All eight of our grandchildren bring us joy that words hardly capture. They are not only building lives for themselves but investing in others.

Each summer, Trent and Wendy's children help Wendy lead Vacation Bible School, guiding younger children in their first steps of faith. Several also volunteer to teach Sunday school.

Our daughter's children have remained active in their parishes, attending mass faithfully and serving in small but regular ways before they left home. Noah continues to seek a church community that fits his current season of life, and I have no doubt God will guide him to the right place.

This is what legacy looks like. It is not static or sentimental. It is alive and moving, passing from one generation to the next. It is faith practiced around breakfast tables, in classrooms, on ballfields, in submarines, and in sanctuaries. It is the intentional, everyday faithfulness that ripples outward far beyond what we can see.

When I look at our daughter's and son's families, I see the evidence of God's hand—steady, patient, and sure. Their story gives me faith for all the stories still unfolding.

Legacy Principles for the Reader

Here's where I want to bring the challenge to you. Each one of us is building a legacy, and as I've had more time recently to consider what my legacy will be, I've identified six principles that I want to encourage you with. I'll list them all up front and then give a few examples of how God has led me to these pieces of wisdom.

Legacy Principle #1

The story of our eight grandchildren shows that legacy is shaped by shared environments and shared practices. Faith isn't passed down by accident; it's reinforced by rhythms like church involvement, Christian education, Vacation Bible School, and consistent modeling at home.

For You: What environments are you intentionally choosing (schools, churches, communities) that will shape your family's faith?

What traditions or habits could you start, like serving together, teaching younger kids, or attending camp, that would leave an imprint on the next generation?

Legacy Principle #2

The story of our daughter's two sons teaches us that legacy includes both the joys and the heartaches of family life. Every family has its Noahs, those who flourish, and its Joshuas, those who struggle. Both are part of the story.

For You: Who in your family is flourishing right now? How can you affirm, celebrate, and encourage them to keep walking in faith?

Who in your family is struggling or drifting? Are you willing to be the steady anchor, praying and waiting patiently until they find their way back?

Legacy is not just about passing on successes; it's about remaining faithful and loving even when the path is uncertain.

Legacy Principle #3

Legacy isn't built only on milestones; it's cemented in daily habits of worship, service, and faithfulness.

For You: What small habits are you modeling that your children or grandchildren might carry on?

If someone looked at your weekly rhythm, what would they assume about your faith priorities?

Legacy Principle #4

Families are God's frontline navigators.

For You: Who are you "keeping watch" for right now?

Is there a family member who needs you to be consistently quietly present and available, waiting for the right time to point them back toward God?

Legacy Principle #5

Every one of us inherits something—habits, values, faith assumptions.

For You: What did you inherit from your family—positive or negative?

How will you strengthen or redirect that inheritance for those who come after you?

Legacy Principle #6

Everyone can leave a legacy artifact a journal, a collection of stories, letters, or a testimony of God's faithfulness.

For You: What could you create that your children and grandchildren would treasure when you are gone?

Faith Passed Down

Scripture speaks of faith being passed "from generation to generation." It is not simply the transfer of information or doctrine, like a textbook handed from one student to another. It is the shaping of a family culture where finding and following God feels natural, expected, and encouraged. In this type of family environment, faith becomes part of the atmosphere, breathed in and lived out until it feels as normal as sunlight and air.

You can see that culture in specific everyday ways. Many of our grandchildren serve in their churches, teaching Sunday school, helping with activities, and volunteering at Vacation Bible School each summer. Their mother, our daughter-in-law Wendy, often directs the program, and the kids rally around her. Together, they make it something joyful and contagious. Watching that happens year after year fills me with immense gratitude.

Another story that captures this generational faith involves Wendy's father, Bill, who was visiting the Young Life camp with his wife, Peggy. Years ago, Tami and I were adult guest hosts at the camp in southern New York along the Delaware River. Among the other guests that week was a couple from Virginia. The wife was a believer, but her husband was not. He had come reluctantly, mostly to please her, and he avoided almost everything about camp. He skipped group meetings, sat alone during free time, and only showed up for meals. You could tell he was miserable and just waiting for the week to end.

At one of the morning meetings, Bill stood up and said he was going fishing that afternoon. Then he asked if anyone wanted to join him. The reluctant husband immediately volunteered. He was eager for any excuse to escape the camp routine and do something that felt normal.

That afternoon, Bill waded with him into the Delaware River, the water up to their chests. As he taught him to fly fish, he started to talk about Jesus. It was not a sermon, just a conversation between two men standing in the current, one teaching the other to cast a line and, at the same time, casting something eternal into the heart of the other.

When they returned from the river, something had changed. The man who had been closed off all week began to smile and join conversations. He attended the next meeting willingly. By the end of camp, he was fully engaged. When he returned home to Virginia, he joined their local Young Life committee and later became its chairman.

I do not know exactly what Bill said that day, but the Lord worked through him. In just one afternoon, a man's life was turned completely around. That moment became part of Bill's legacy, a story that continues to inspire both of our families.

It also reminds me that faith is rarely passed down through big speeches or formal lessons. It often happens quietly, in ordinary moments that turn sacred. A man teaches another man to fish, a parent reads Scripture to a child, a grandparent offers a prayer. These small acts form the current that carries faith forward.

I can see how God has used people like Bill, and so many others in my family, to shape my faith. Each one has been a waypoint on my map, helping me find direction when I needed it most.

That is the beauty of generational faith. It does not chain us to the past; it moves us forward. It connects us through time, linking one life of trust to another, all the way back to the heart of God.

Family Navigation in Scripture

God has been using families to navigate individuals to Himself since the beginning of time. The story of Moses is one of the clearest examples. When Pharaoh ordered that every Hebrew baby boy be killed, Moses' mother refused to surrender to fear. She placed her son in a basket and set him afloat on the Nile, trusting that God would somehow guide him. Yet she did not simply let him go but sent his sister, Miriam to stay close by hiding along the riverbank to keep watch over the drifting basket.

When Pharaoh's daughter found the baby and was moved with compassion, Miriam stepped out of hiding. With remarkable courage and presence of mind, she offered to find a Hebrew woman to nurse the child—and brought their own mother to take that role. The story looks miraculous, but it also shows a family working faithfully within God's providence.

That is what family does at its best. It stands guard at the edges of danger. It steps forward at the right moment with words that restore identity and belonging. Miriam on the riverbank is every parent who prays late into the night, every sibling who refuses to give up, every grandparent who seriously believes that God will bring their loved one home.

Early Influences and Legacy

Faith did not begin with me. It was already part of my family's story long before I was born. My mother grew up in a family of twelve children. They were not Catholic, but they were deeply Christian. On Sunday mornings, some of them walked to the Baptist church at one end of the street, while others went to the Methodist church on the other. It didn't matter which one they chose. Faith was part of the air they breathed. Church was not a debate. It was a given.

One of the greatest influences on my life was my uncle, who became like a second father to me. He was a carpenter by trade, a hunter and fisherman by choice, and a gas station owner by necessity. What stood out about him was his quiet consistency. He lived his faith without fanfare. He did not talk much about God, but his life spoke clearly.

I can still picture him in his workshop, hands calloused, sawdust floating in the air, humming an old hymn as he worked. When he became ill with cancer, I stayed with him during his final days. He is the one to whom I read Psalm 23 aloud in his last moments on earth. I wasn't sure if it was appropriate at the time, but it felt right. The familiar words, "The LORD is my shepherd, I shall not want," filled the room with a peace that settled over both of us.

That moment marked me in ways I did not understand then. His faith, lived so quietly, became part of mine. His patience and integrity left an imprint on my soul. Looking back now, I can see that what I learned from him was not just how to live well, but how to die with peace and trust in God.

The Christmas Book Mission

One of my goals is to write a Christmas book, partly as a surprise gift for my family and partly as a resource for others who might find themselves searching for direction. I picture it as a kind of navigation log, a record of the journeys we have taken together and the faithfulness of God that has guided us through each one.

It is not about being remembered but about leaving behind something useful that might steady the next generation when I am no longer here to answer their questions. God has been so faithful in so many situations and I want to pass along every story, every lesson, every testimony of God's grace because they will become stars to steer by.

If this book helps even one person find their bearings when life feels dark or uncertain, then it will have done its work. That is the mission.

Navigation Callout: Polynesian Wayfinders and Generational Wisdom

For thousands of years Polynesian navigators made epic voyages across the open Pacific ocean. They sailed hundreds, even thousands, of miles between islands, guided only by what they carried in memory and practice.

The key was that this wisdom was passed down from generation to generation. Fathers taught sons how to read the stars, how a cluster like Pleiades rose in a certain season and set in another. Mothers sang songs that encoded distances between islands and the patterns of swells. Older navigators trained younger ones to notice the flight paths of seabirds, the feel of the current against a canoe, the changing colors of the water over a reef. Navigation wasn't an individual skill; it was a family culture.

That's why the knowledge endured. Each generation inherited not just information, but a way of life. The young learned by watching, listening, and practicing alongside their elders until the wisdom became second nature. A skilled wayfinder carried with them knowledge from the generations of navigators who had sailed before.

In the same way, faith and values are transmitted from one generation to the next. Often through families. This looks like parents who pray, grandparents who tell stories of God's faithfulness, and siblings who encourage one another in faith. All of these create a "wayfinding culture" where understanding how to navigate the spiritual life is the natural thing to do. Just as Polynesian families prepared their children to cross oceans they themselves might never see, our calling is to prepare the next generation to navigate seas we may never sail.

The Anchor Holds

We all walk a different path, but what a gift it is to leave a legacy of a strong anchor that holds fast. Our calling as parents and grandparents is to be the steady point when other compasses spin, to hold fast when the waters are uncertain.

Now, in my battle with cancer, I'm paying careful attention to how this will take place in the future of my family. I see the ways my children are guiding their children. My grandchildren are raising the next generation. Even my great-grandchild is being nurtured in faith. The voyage continues. The compass still points true. The anchor holds.

I'd like to close this chapter with a testimony my grandson made for an FCA (Fellowship of Christian Athletes) video. His words warm our hearts and capture what I'm trying to say quite well:

Brett Gladstone's Testimony

What's up guys, my name is Brett Gladstone. I go to Grove City College. I'm a senior, I play lacrosse (midfield).

I grew up in Baltimore, Maryland. I went to Mary Church High School, and I'm going to tell you a little bit about my story.

I really wanted to make the varsity team my freshman year of high school, and I placed a lot of my identity in who I was as a lacrosse player. So when I did not make the varsity team my freshman year, it kind of devastated me. That pushed me to work really hard and do all the things the coaches said to make varsity the next year.

The next year rolls around—I don't make it again. And it was a devastating hit on me because I placed a lot of my identity in who I was, in how people looked at me as a person. When I didn't make the team, I didn't really have anything to turn to, because all of my cards were in lacrosse.

After I didn't make the team, I had an awesome conversation with my dad. He sat me down and was like, "Brett, your identity isn't in who you are as a lacrosse player. It's in who Jesus Christ has you to be throughout your life." That was just a very impactful statement. My dad said it—I've heard it so many times—but until what I had my identity in failed, I didn't really get the big picture.

Another thing that helped me in my life in high school was Young Life. My dad introduced me to Young Life when I was really young, and I've been around it all my life. I've been to many camps and stuff like that, but it just really helped me make my faith my own.

It also showed me that Jesus Christ is the only fulfillment I need. I don't need it in lacrosse. I don't need it in school or anything else. You can find fulfillment in Christ.

Continuing on in high school, lacrosse definitely changed for me. I just saw it in a different way. Now it wasn't the thing at the forefront of my life. It helped me play with a lot more freedom, with God at the center. It just helped me play with a lot more fun, really, because lacrosse just wasn't the thing giving me fulfillment anymore.

I was blessed enough to be able to go to Grove City College. One of the reasons I chose the school was because of the people there. They had a club lacrosse program at the time, and they were transitioning into varsity. But the people there weren't there just to play lacrosse—they were there to follow God and build relationships and have that awesome community. That's one of the reasons I chose Grove City.

Going to Grove City allowed me to apply for the 2019 FCA internship. I was fortunate enough to actually get the internship, and throughout that summer God taught me how important community is—being with other like-minded individuals who love God and want to grow in their faith together.

That summer was one of the best summers of my life. Not only was I growing in my faith, but I was also growing in relationships with other people who shared a common goal and a common identity in Christ.

Sometimes it's hard for me to put into words all the things God is doing in my life. But I know He has me here for a reason. I think some of those reasons could be to help lead the other guys on the team. I'm a senior, I've been through college, and I kind of know what it's like. So I can help those guys lead through college.

I think another reason is that He just wants me to help others, because others have helped me. Throughout my college career, I've had awesome guys in my life who've shown me what it means to be a man of God—really putting faith at the forefront of my life.

The last thing is just to share the love I've received throughout my life—from my dad, my mom, my siblings, FCA, Grove City, my coaches, my teammates. All of that—just to be a light for Jesus Christ for anyone watching this.

I just want you guys to know: put God first in your life. Lacrosse may seem awesome now, sports may seem awesome now—but when they eventually don't work out, or when you can't play anymore, what are you going to turn your faith to? What are you going to put your trust in?

I just want you guys to know that you are loved by your Creator. Put your faith in Jesus Christ, because He brings satisfaction, and He brings fulfillment.

Part Five

Helping Others Find Their Way

Chapter 16

Sharing Our Path With Those Who Come Behind

 Let your light shine before others, so that they may see your good works and give glory to your Father who is in heaven.

— Matthew 5:16

Through forty years of serving on Young Life committees, I've learned something fundamental about spiritual navigation: It's meant to be shared. All of the lessons God teaches us, the storms we weather, the ways our lives get changed and redirected aren't just meant to teach us but intended for us to use as encouragement to others. Other travelers will navigate similar waters that we have faced and God wants to use what He has given each one of us.

I've discovered that our most difficult navigation challenges often qualify us to guide others through theirs.

The Accidental Guide

I never set out to be a spiritual guide. After our son's transformation at Young Life, Tami and I simply wanted to support the organization that had so profoundly impacted our family. We joined committees, helped with fundraising, attended events, and housed several Young Life leaders over the years. We thought we were just volunteers, supporters from the sidelines.

But Young Life has a way of drawing you deeper. Without meaning to, we'd become guides, not in any formal capacity, but simply by being present, by sharing our story, by supporting the mission that had changed our son's life.

The interesting thing about becoming a guide is that you rarely feel qualified. I'd think, "What do I have to offer? I'm just a guy who worked in intelligence and contracts, who made plenty of mistakes, who's still figuring things out myself." But that's exactly what qualifies us. Not perfection, but the journey itself.

Sharing Along the Way

Remember Tom Neary, my dear friend and mentor from the Air Force years? Our paths stayed connected through retirement and we shared many what I'd call "joyful in hope" moments. In 2013, both of our families met for a week at the Neary cabin on Coeur d'Alene Lake in Idaho. There were thirty-two of us all together. Each day we set aside time for prayer and reflection. We didn't have a program to follow but enjoyed that time simply as families considering God's work in our lives over the years. It was ordinary and holy at the same time.

Not long after, Tom was diagnosed with ALS and later went home to be with the Lord. Joan, his wife, and their children and grandchildren cared for him with a grace that never lost sight of God. Neither Tom nor Joan surrendered their faith through that agonizing season. When I delivered the eulogy at Tom's funeral, I experienced again the way Christ guides thoughts and sentiments when human words fall short. The Neary family, very much like mine, centers life on Christ, and their witness continues to strengthen my faith even now.

Tom taught me many things in a professional sense and he also modeled for me lessons I carry which help me as I try to guide others on this spiritual journey. He showed me that simply being there, praying, listening, and reflecting, often guides others through difficulty more than any speech. God continued to use His mannerisms even when ALS stole away his physical abilities. When Tom could not really talk anymore, he still had that Tom Neary smile that showed his continued gratitude and faith in God even during his final days.

If I have helped anyone find their bearings, it's in part because Tom helped me find mine. His mentorship, which was steady and Christ-centered, remains one of the clearest examples in my life of how God uses His people to guide each other.

The Unexpected Ministry of Weakness

During the four months when I was recovering from the fall from my roof, God allowed me to minister to people that I would likely not have had the same connection with if my body wasn't in a state of weakness. As I lived that time completely dependent on others, I found myself in conversations with people facing their own limitations. They didn't want to hear from someone who had it all together. They needed to hear from someone who understood what it was like to not be able to tie your own shoes, to need help with basic tasks, to wrestle with the loss of independence.

The broken places in our journey, the failures, the falls, the times we got completely lost, these often become the very experiences that qualify us to guide others. Not because we emerged unscathed, but because we learned what it takes to navigate with a limp.

Cancer as Navigation Credential

Because I've been on this pancreatic cancer journey for some time, I'm now qualified as a guide over this difficult terrain. Not that I've taken some course in cancer management or an intensive study in God's presence in hard times, but because I've lived just a little longer than someone being diagnosed today with the same uncertain prognosis. Of course I don't have all of the answers. Certainly I'm not handling this experience perfectly. But honestly, I'm figuring out this path, and others need to know it can be walked.

At the treatment center, conversations happen naturally. We share diagnoses, compare treatments, exchange fears and hopes. Without meaning to, we become guides for each other. The shared experience creates instant connection and credibility. There's something about sitting in adjacent chemotherapy chairs that strips away pretense and creates space for truth.

Here's just one example. A woman I met there, maybe ten years younger than me, had just received her diagnosis. The fear in her eyes was familiar. I didn't try to comfort her with platitudes or promise her it would be easy. Instead, I told her what I was learning: that you can be terrified and faithful at the same time. That some treatments work better than others. That it's okay to cry in the parking lot. That your people will show up in ways that surprise you.

When someone newly diagnosed wants to know how to keep faith through this, I don't give them a theological treatise. I tell them the truth: some days faith feels strong, other days it doesn't. But I keep doing the faithful things, praying even when it feels empty, reading Scripture even when it seems distant, accepting help from church friends even when I'd rather be alone. The feelings come and go. The practices keep me anchored.

Somehow, in the middle of my own struggle, I am confident that God is using and will continue to use even this. My cancer isn't wasted. My weakness isn't disqualifying. It's exactly what qualifies me as a guide.

The Compass Points You Share

God has taught me a lot of lessons in my long life of walking with Him. I am still learning more, but with every new encounter of someone needing encouragement and hope, I am grateful for the ways God continuously fed me spiritual truth throughout the years. It is a gift to have experienced so much godly teaching and mentorship in my life-time and I see now that God intended for me to take in real-life under-standing of Him in order for me to share it with others. Guiding others doesn't require having all the answers. It requires having a few reliable compass points you can share. I've alluded to these lessons throughout this book, but I'd like to share them again in this context of sharing as a guide to others.

God Is Faithful Even When He Feels Absent

This might be the most important navigation truth I can share, because everyone eventually faces seasons when God seems to have disap-peared. I can speak to this with authority, not the authority of theolog-ical training, but the authority of experience.

In Vietnam, when military conflict was close at hand and I was scared to death, God felt absent. I went to chapel, said the prayers, but felt nothing. The physical threats were real, the fear was constant, and heaven seemed locked to communicating with me. During those years when I was searching for my purpose, wondering why God had put me on earth, I'd ask, sometimes beg, for direction, and hear only echoes. Even now, some days during chemotherapy, I feel like I'm talking to an empty room when I pray. The words go up and seem to hit the ceiling.

But I'm confident God's presence isn't dependent on my ability to sense it.

Looking back on Vietnam, I can see His protection. I lived through close calls that weren't quite as close as they could have been. No doubt decisions that I made which seemed minor likely kept me safe when I didn't even realize it. Thinking on my purpose-searching years, I can see He was preparing me to understand that family was my calling.

When I share this compass point with others, I don't minimize their experience of God's absence. I validate it. "Yes, sometimes God feels completely gone. I've been there. I know that hollow echo. But He's still there, still working, still faithful. You just can't see it yet."

This isn't platitude. It's my testimony backed by decades of evidence. It's what I wish someone had told me in Vietnam.

Failure Isn't Final

My missile field demotion in 1973 should have ended my Air Force career. I failed completely and was swiftly relieved from duty and demoted to deputy crew commander. In military culture, that kind of failure typically means you're done. The black mark follows you. The reputation sticks.

But within three years, I was representing my wing at Olympic Arena, the premier missile combat competition.

When I share this with someone facing career failure, I don't minimize the pain or the fear. I remember driving home that night in Montana, convinced everything was over. My shame was suffocating. The future looked blank. But I emphasize what happened next, the mentors who appeared, the slow rebuilding of competence, the eventual triumph that seemed impossible from that moment of failure. The way God used even that humiliation to strip away pride and rebuild something stronger.

The key truth here isn't that everything will work out perfectly. Sometimes it doesn't. Sometimes careers don't recover. Sometimes marriages don't heal. Sometimes the prodigal doesn't come home. But the truth is that failure isn't the end of your story. It might be the end of a chapter, but there are more chapters to write. God specializes in resurrection, in bringing life from death, success from failure, purpose from pain.

I've seen this principle work beyond career failures. Broken marriages that got restored after years of hard work and grace. Prodigals who came home when everyone had given up hope. Addictions that were overcome through community and stubborn faith. Failure feels final in the moment, but it rarely is. This compass point gives people hope to keep navigating when they think they've hit a dead end.

People Are God's Primary Delivery System

This compass point surprises people, especially those waiting for God to show up in dramatic, supernatural ways. But in my experience, God almost always shows up through people.

After my missile field failure, God showed up as Air Force mentors who invested in a failed officer when they had every reason to write me off. After my fall from the roof, God showed up as family members who helped me with basic tasks without complaint, as medical professionals who aided my recovery with skill and patience, as friends who kept my spirits up during the long, humiliating months of dependence. During cancer, God is showing up as oncology nurses who remember my name and my story, as church friends and neighbors who bring meals I didn't ask for but gratefully receive, as prayer warriors interceding on my behalf when I'm too tired to pray for myself.

When someone says, "I'm praying for God to help," I often respond, "Look around. He's probably already sending help through people. Who's showing up in your life right now?"

It's amazing how often they realize that the colleague who keeps offering to listen, the neighbor who brings unexpected casseroles, the old friend who suddenly reconnects after years of silence, these are

God's delivery system in action. Not coincidences. Providence with a human face.

This compass point helps people recognize divine provision that doesn't look divine. It looks like ordinary people doing ordinary kindness. But that's how God works most of the time, through human hands, human voices, human presence.

Your Purpose Might Be Simpler Than You Think

I spent years agonizing over my purpose, certain God had some grand mission for me that I was somehow missing. I prayed, searched, worried that I wasn't doing enough, and wasn't fulfilling whatever calling God had for me. The anxiety about purpose became its own burden. I'd look at other people who seemed to have clear callings, dramatic testimonies, obvious ministries, and wonder what I was missing.

Then it dawned on me, gradually, as my children started having children: my purpose was simply to build and nurture a faithful family. Not to change the world, not to achieve something spectacular, but to raise children who knew God, who would raise children who knew God. To be present. To be faithful. To pass on what matters.

When I share this compass point, I often see relief wash over people's faces. They've been torturing themselves trying to discover some elaborate calling, when their purpose might be beautifully simple: be a good spouse, raise faithful children, do honest work, serve your church, love your neighbors.

Jesus said the greatest commandments were to love God and love others. Sometimes our purpose is just that straightforward. We complicate it because simple feels insufficient, but God often works through the beautifully ordinary. The daily, unglamorous faithfulness. The small obediences no one sees. This compass point gives people permission to stop searching for the spectacular and start investing in the obvious.

The Practices Matter More Than the Feelings

This might be the most practical compass point I share. Faith isn't primarily about feeling God's presence or experiencing spiritual highs.

Faith is about regular spiritual practices, prayer, Scripture reading, church attendance, and service, that we maintain regardless of feelings.

During my year in Vietnam, I felt nothing when I went to chapel, but I kept going. Sat in the same pew. Said the same prayers. Went through the motions when motion. During the dark season of searching for purpose, prayer felt pointless, but I kept praying. Words into the void, over and over. During chemotherapy, when the drugs make everything feel foggy and distant, I still maintain the practices.

Why? Because these practices are navigation instruments. When pilots fly through clouds, they can't trust their feelings. Their inner ear might tell them they're climbing when they're actually diving. Spatial disorientation kills. They have to trust their instruments, the altimeter, the compass, the artificial horizon, even when every instinct screams something different.

When someone says, "I don't feel God anymore," I share this compass point: "Keep doing the faithful things anyway. Feelings come and go. The practices keep you oriented." The practices kept me pointed in the right direction throughout life until the fog lifted.

Listen More than You Speak

This goes against every instinct when someone comes to you for guidance. You want to share everything you know, solve their problems, and provide answers. But I've learned that people often know their own answers. They just need someone to help them articulate them.

When someone facing cancer asks me how to handle the fear, my first response isn't to launch into my story. It's to ask, "What specifically are you afraid of?" Then I listen. Really listen. Not just waiting for my turn to talk, but listening to understand. I watch their faces and hear what they're not saying. Often, in the process of explaining their fear to me, they begin to understand it themselves. The act of being heard creates clarity.

Active listening also helps you provide relevant guidance. The person afraid of leaving their family financially vulnerable needs different compass points than the person afraid of physical pain. The person wrestling with "why me?" needs different navigation help than the person wrestling with "what's next?" You can't know which compass points to share until you've really heard where they are.

Listening also builds trust. When people feel truly heard, they're more likely to receive whatever guidance you eventually offer. They know you understand their specific situation, not just their general category of struggle. You've earned the right to speak into their life because you've first honored their experience.

Share Stories, Not Advice

When someone's struggling with career failure, I don't tell them what to do.

First, stories are non-threatening. Advice can feel like judgment: "You should do this" implies they're not doing it right. But a story is just a story where I get to tell the things I've experienced and learned. The listener can take what applies and leave what doesn't without feeling criticized.

Second, stories are memorable. People might forget your three-point plan for dealing with failure, but they'll remember the image of a demoted officer eventually representing his wing at competition. They'll remember the guy who couldn't tie his shoes for six months but learned about grace through dependence. Stories stick in ways that principles don't.

Third, stories provide hope through example. When I share about recovering from career failure, I'm not just telling them it's possible. I'm proving it's possible. The story itself is evidence that this storm can be weathered.

Finally, stories allow people to draw their own applications. What helped me might not help them in exactly the same way, but they can extract the principles that apply to their situation. They become active participants in their own navigation rather than passive recipients of advice. They own the insight because they discovered it through your story.

Admit What You Don't Know

This might be the most important skill for building trust as a guide. The most dangerous guides are those who pretend to know everything, who have an answer for every question, who never acknowledge uncertainty. They project confidence but create distance.

When someone asks me, "Why did God allow this cancer?" I tell them honestly: "I don't know. I've wondered the same thing. In fact, I'm still wondering. But here's what I do know..." Then I share what I've learned about God's faithfulness in the midst of not understanding.

"I don't know" is often the most helpful thing you can say, especially when followed by, "but let's figure it out together." This transforms you from an expert dispensing wisdom to a fellow traveler sharing the journey. It makes you safe, approachable, and human. Someone who won't judge them for their own doubts and questions.

Admitting ignorance also protects people from bad guidance. I don't know everything about cancer treatment, so I don't pretend that I do. I share my experience but encourage them to talk to their doctors. I don't understand all of God's ways, so I don't manufacture explanations for suffering. Theological formulas would insult their pain so I point to what I do know.

The questions without answers don't threaten my faith anymore. They're just part of the territory. And admitting that makes me a better guide.

Point to True North, Not to Yourself

A guide's job is to help others find God, not to become their god. The best guides work themselves out of a job because they help the next person understand how to navigate.

When someone thanks me for helping them through a difficult season, I'm careful to redirect: "I'm glad God used our conversation. He's the one who got you through." This isn't false humility. It's accurate theology. I might be a navigation aid, but God is the Navigator. I'm just one instrument in His toolkit.

This also means encouraging people to develop their own connection with God rather than depending on mine. When I share the things I've learned, it's always with the goal of helping the next person recognize God's work in their own life. Teach them to read their own spiritual maps, to recognize their own compass points, to hear God's voice for themselves.

Sometimes this means stepping back when you want to step forward. When someone starts depending too heavily on your guidance, it might be time to create some distance, to encourage them to seek God directly. To pray more than they text you. To listen for God's voice before asking for yours. The goal isn't to create followers but to develop fellow navigators who can then help others find their way.

The best moment as a guide isn't when someone thanks you for your wisdom. It's when someone says, "I've been helping someone else through what I went through, sharing what you shared with me." That's when you know you've pointed them to True North rather than to yourself.

The Privilege of Proximity

Sometimes being a guide is simply about proximity. You happen to be the Christian in the cancer ward. You happen to be the experienced person in the office. You happen to be the one who's walked this particular path before. Suddenly you're the guide whether you planned to be or not.

During my intelligence work, both in the Air Force and later as a contractor, I often found myself working with people who had no faith background. Not because I sought them out, but because that's who was there. Proximity created many opportunities for conversations about life, purpose, and faith. These natural discussions arose from working together through late nights, stressful missions, coffee breaks. The everyday rhythms created openness.

Leaving a Legacy

Navigation is never just about today's journey. It's about the map we leave behind.

When I set the goal to finish this book by Christmas, it wasn't only about checking off a project. It was about legacy. I wanted my family, and anyone who might read this book, to have a map that pointed to True North. Not a map to me. Not even a map of my exact journey. But a map showing that True North exists. That it holds. That you can navigate by it through any storm.

Legacy isn't about recognition. It's not about having your name remembered or getting credit for what you've done. It's about remaining faithful until God calls us home. About finishing what God gave you to do.

As Paul declared near the end of his life: "I have fought the good fight, I have finished the race, I have kept the faith" (2 Timothy 4:7).

That is the legacy worth leaving and what I want my grandchildren to remember. Not that their grandfather was perfect. That he was faithful. That when storms came, he didn't abandon ship. And that True North held.

Navigation Callout: The Map That Changed the World

In 1815, William Smith published the first geological map of Britain. This wasn't the first geological map, but it was the first to cover such a large area in great detail. Smith had no formal geological training. But he noticed something others had missed: rock layers appeared in predictable patterns across the countryside. For years, he traveled Britain on horseback, documenting formations, collecting samples, and making observations. He faced skepticism from the scientific establishment. Who was this working-class surveyor to challenge accepted wisdom? He went bankrupt funding his research and even spent time in debtor's prison. But he kept deterred.

When he finally published his geological map it was massive, over eight feet tall, hand-colored, showing rock strata across England, Wales, and part of Scotland. Smith's observations and years of research emphasized that rock layers can be dated by their fossils. His careful observations reshaped how scientists understood the earth and predicted where to find coal, iron, and building stone. This understanding led to modern geology and developed a new understanding of how to understand geological time.

Your life is a map, too. What map will you leave behind? It might not look like an eight foot colorful chart of rock formations, but it will tell a story. Perhaps it will be a faithful marriage, a mentoring relationship, a quiet act of service, or simply a consistent walk with God that others could follow. Whatever it looks like, your map matters.

Reflection and Application

The race is not finished. The map of your life is still being drawn. You can't control every bend in the road, but you can choose how you walk it—eyes fixed on Jesus, compass set by the Spirit, guided by the Word, and surrounded by a community of fellow travelers.

So chart your course forward with courage. Run your race with endurance. Fight the good fight. Leave a map that points others to True North.

- **Reflect:** Which of the navigation tools—Scripture, prayer, reflection, worship, community—do you need to strengthen most in this season? Where have you seen them already at work in your story?
- **Act:** Choose one practice and commit to it daily for the next 30 days. Share your plan with someone in your navigation community for accountability.
- **Pray:** *Lord, keep me oriented to You. Teach me to use the tools You've given—Your Word, prayer, reflection, and community— to chart a faithful course. Help me leave behind a map that points others to Jesus, my True North. Amen.*

Chapter 17

The Journey Continues

 I have fought the good fight, I have finished the race, I
have kept the faith.

— 2 Timothy 4:7

In 1519, Ferdinand Magellan set out with five ships and a bold
dream: to sail around the world. It was a journey no one had
completed before. No one even knew for certain it could be done.
The maps were incomplete. The risks were extraordinary. Many
thought he was mad.

Three years later, only one ship returned to Spain, battered, leaking,
barely seaworthy, but triumphant. The first circumnavigation of the
globe. Proof that the world was round. Proof that the Pacific could be
crossed. Proof that what seemed impossible was merely unprecedented.

Magellan wasn't on board. He died in the Philippines in 1521, two
years into the voyage, killed in battle on the island of Mactan. He'd
survived storms, starvation, mutiny, and uncharted waters, only to fall
on a beach thousands of miles from home.

Juan Sebastián Elcano, captained the one surviving ship which
made the final leg of the journey back to Spain. At that point the crew
was decimated. Only 18 of the original 237 men completed the voyage.

They faced starvation, scurvy, hostile waters, and the constant threat of death. Ships had been lost. Men had died. The leader was gone. Magellan never finished the journey. But the remnant of his crew did. His vision outlived him and his goal became their mission.

When they finally reached Spain in September 1522, the single surviving ship, the Victoria, was falling apart. The men were skeletal, sick, exhausted. But they'd done it. They'd circled the globe. And Magellan's name, though he never finished the voyage, became forever linked with one of history's greatest journeys.

That's the story of faith too. We all reach the point where we hand the journey over to others to carry on. What matters then is how well we've prepared our crew to continue.

Your Life as an Ever-Expanding Map

I'm acutely aware that my map will remain unfinished. There are conversations I won't have, lessons I won't teach, moments I won't witness. Grandchildren's graduations I might miss. Weddings I might not attend. The Christmas book I want to write will get written, but I have no guarantee I'll be there to see it published. The wisdom I hope to pass on might remain partially unspoken.

That's the nature of every human journey. Cancer just sets a timeline that has to be confronted.

The truth is, no one is guaranteed even another minute. The healthy forty-year-old walking out the door this morning might not come home tonight. The retirement you're planning for might never arrive. The book you'll write someday might never get written. We're all living on borrowed time.

Like Magellan, each of us leaves unfinished work. Projects incomplete. Relationships not fully healed. Growth not fully realized. That's not failure. That's humanity.

Abraham "went out, not knowing where he was going" (Hebrews 11:8), and died still longing for the city God promised. He never saw the fulfillment of God's promise that his descendants would be as numerous as the stars. He never saw the nations God promised that would descend from him and never experienced the way His family would become a blessing to all peoples. His map was wildly incomplete.

Moses led God's people through forty years of wilderness wandering, received the Law, and managed the grumbling group of former slaves. But he died on Mount Nebo, looking at the Promised Land from a distance. He could see it. But God said, "This far, no farther." It was Joshua and the next generation who crossed over. Moses' map ended at the Jordan River, but the journey didn't. The people he'd led for forty years continued without him.

Paul admitted near the end of his life, "Not that I...am already perfect, but I press on" (Philippians 3:12). Even the great apostle, writer of much of the New Testament, planter of churches across the Roman world, acknowledged his map was incomplete. There were churches he wanted to visit but couldn't. Letters he wanted to write but didn't. Disciples he wanted to train but wouldn't have time for. He left goals and work unfinished.

The Bible is full of leaders who never saw the whole map completed, but faithfully walked their part of the journey and passed it on. David gathered materials for the temple but Solomon built it. John the Baptist prepared the way but didn't see the resurrection. Prophets spoke of a Messiah they'd never meet. Each played their part in a journey larger than any individual life.

That's the pattern. Not completion, but faithfulness. Not seeing the whole map, but walking your part of it well. Not finishing everything, but finishing what God gave you to do.

Your map will be unfinished. So will mine. The question is: will it be faithful? Will it point others toward True North even after you're gone? Will your crew be able to pick it up and continue the journey?

That's what matters. Not how much you completed, but how well you prepared others to continue. Not how far you got, but whether you stayed on course. Not whether you saw the Promised Land, but whether you kept walking toward it.

Magellan died halfway around the world. But his name became synonymous with exploration, with courage, with the audacity to attempt what no one thought possible.

Your name might not end up in history books. But it will be written on hearts. On the lives you've touched. On the map you've left for those who follow.

And that's a legacy worth leaving.

Navigation Callout: Captain James Cook

In the 1700s, Captain James Cook set out to chart the uncharted. His voyages took him to New Zealand, the eastern coast of Australia, and deep into the Pacific. He mapped more of the world than almost any sailor before him.

But Cook never finished his final journey. In 1779, he was killed in Hawaii during a clash with islanders. His mapping ambitions were left incomplete. And yet, the charts he created were so precise that sailors used them for more than a hundred years. Long after Cook was gone, his work guided ships safely through waters he would never sail again.

Cook's life's work and lasting influence as a navigator show that God's plan does not mean that we will experience all of the things we set out to accomplish, but we can focus and be intentional to leave maps that are clear enough for others to follow.

Preparing the Crew

My crew is my family. Tami, my partner for over sixty years. Through Air Force moves, Pentagon pressures, career transitions, a roof fall, and now cancer. She's been the steady presence, the one who kept navigating when I couldn't see straight.

Our daughter, steady in her Catholic faith, growing deeper with each passing year. Not flashy. Not loud. Just faithful. Showing up. Raising her kids with the same compass pointing to God as the True North which is what we tried to give her.

Our son, transformed by Young Life, who served on staff for thirteen years. Watching him lead kids through the same transformation he experienced, confirmed that God was continuing to lead my children along their paths as He did for me.

Our eight grandchildren, each finding their own way while using the family map pointing to God which we've tried to provide. Some are farther along than others. Some are still figuring out which direction is North. But they all know the path and understand our confidence that God is real.

I think of our grandson in the Navy, training for nuclear submarines. He's navigating literal oceans while navigating spiritual ones too. His efforts require discipline and precision in the middle of high stakes. Everything about submarine duty requires trust in instruments when you can't see. That's faith training, whether he knows it or not.

I think of our struggling grandson, eighteen and in rehabilitation. His map is harder to read right now. The path is unclear. The destination is uncertain. But the family map is still there when he's ready to use it. We're praying. We're present. We're not giving up. And neither is God.

I think of our oldest granddaughter with her new baby. She's beginning to draw maps for the next generation. Teaching her daughter the same truths her parents taught her. The same prayers. The same songs. The journey to the North Star continues.

At Tami's eightieth birthday celebration, surrounded by children, grandchildren and great-grandchild, our daughter stood and read aloud words that felt like they were meant not only for her mother, but for all of us. For our whole family. For our legacy. For this book. For everything we've tried to build and pass on.

She read from Ephesians 3:12–19 in the NIV:

 In him and through faith in him we may approach God with freedom and confidence. I ask you, therefore, not to be discouraged because of my sufferings for you, which are your glory.

For this reason I kneel before the Father, from whom every family in heaven and on earth derives its name. I pray that out of his glorious riches he may strengthen you with power through his Spirit in your inner being, so that Christ may dwell in your hearts through faith. And I pray that you, being rooted and established in love, may have power, together with all the Lord's holy people, to grasp how wide and long and high and deep is the love of Christ, and to know this love that surpasses knowledge— that you may be filled to the measure of all the fullness of God.

After she finished reading, the room was quiet. Tami was crying. So was I. Not sad tears. Grateful tears. Because those words captured everything we'd tried to do for sixty years. Everything we'd tried to build. Everything we'd tried to pass on.

I realized this passage was a compass in itself. They are a guide to the map that we want to leave behind, our legacy.

These words of Paul summarize everything I want to leave behind: confidence to approach God, not cowering but bold because of Christ. Strength in the Spirit when our own strength fails. Christ dwelling in our hearts through faith. Roots sunk deep in love, so deep that storms can't uproot us. And the astonishing, incomprehensible reality of Christ's love that surpasses knowledge. Love which is too wide to measure. Too long to trace. Too high to climb. Too deep to fathom.

That is the map I want my crew to carry forward. If they have that compass, they can navigate anything. Any storm. Any loss. Any confusion. Any darkness.

And when I'm gone, when my part of the map is complete, they'll keep going. They'll add their own sections. Their own discoveries. Their own hard-won wisdom.

And maybe, generations from now, someone will look back and see a family that stayed on course. Not because we were perfect navigators. But because we had a reliable compass.

And we passed it on.

The Unfinished Business of Faith

There's something liberating about accepting that your map will be incomplete. It takes away the impossible pressure of trying to accomplish everything, to solve every problem, to reach every destination, to tie up every loose end. Instead, you focus on faithful navigation for the portion of the journey that's yours.

I think about the things I wanted to do but won't. Long conversations with grandchildren I might not have. Deep talks about life and faith and what matters. Anniversaries with Tami we might not celebrate. Sixty years together, but maybe not seventy. Places we planned to visit. That trip to Ireland we kept postponing. Books I wanted to read and write. The stack on my nightstand keeps growing, but my energy for reading keeps shrinking.

The list of unfinished business grows as my energy for finishing shrinks. Projects half-done. Relationships not fully reconciled. Goals not quite reached. Words not yet spoken.

Some days the unfinished parts frustrate me. I want more time. More energy. More opportunities. I want to finish what I started. I want to see how things turn out. I want to hold that great-great-grandchild. I want to know how my struggling grandson made it through. I want to be there for moments I'll miss.

But this is human. Every navigator eventually reaches the edge of their own map. No one finishes everything. What matters isn't completing everything but navigating faithfully the portion entrusted to you.

Hebrews 11, often called the "Hall of Faith," makes this point powerfully. After listing all these heroes of faith, Abraham, Moses, David, and others, the author concludes: "And all these, having obtained a good testimony through faith, did not receive the promise, God having provided something better for us, that they should not be made perfect apart from us" (Hebrews 11:39-40 NKJV).

God continued to give faith to the descendants of these great men and women. Their unfinished position became starting points for the next generation of navigators. What looked incomplete in one life became the foundation for the next. The journey didn't end. It expanded.

That's the economy of faith. Nothing is wasted. Every incomplete journey contributes to the larger voyage. Every unfinished map helps someone else navigate farther. The incompleteness isn't failure. It's an invitation. Come, continue what we started.

Legacy as an Ongoing Voyage

This book is part of that legacy. It is my way of charting a path for those who come behind me. Not because I've reached the end, not because I have all the answers, but because I want to leave markers for the crew that follows. My goal has been to show where I went, what I found, and where True North held steady.

Every story I've shared, the missile field failure, the roof fall, Vietnam, the Pentagon struggles, the cancer journey, these aren't just my stories anymore. They're navigation markers for my family and for you, the reader. They're saying: "I faced this storm and survived. Here's how

I navigated through it. Here's where I found God in the darkness. Here's where the compass held true."

When my grandchildren face failure and physical limitations, and they will, I want them to know their grandfather failed too. I failed hard, got demoted, and thought my career was over. When I fell off a roof I couldn't tie my own shoes, had to accept help, and learned about grace through dependence. But no matter what happened I kept going, found redemption, and learned that failure and physical limitations aren't final.

I want my children and grandchildren to know that when any of them face their own dark night, and they will, I want them to know I had mine too. In Vietnam. In the search for purpose. In the chemotherapy chair. And True North held; God was faithful even when He felt absent.

Paul's words in 2 Timothy 4:7 give me hope: "I have fought the good fight, I have finished the race, I have kept the faith."

Notice he doesn't say he mapped the whole world or solved every problem or reached every goal. He simply remained faithful. That is the navigator's task: Stay true to True North, and trust the crew to continue the mission. Fight your fight. Finish your race. Keep your faith. That's enough.

Paul then adds something crucial:

> Henceforth there is laid up for me the crown of righteousness, which the Lord, the righteous judge, will award to me on that day, and not only to me but also to all who have loved his appearing.
>
> — 2 Timothy 4:8

The journey continues beyond our path on this earth. There's a final destination that makes every unfinished earthly journey complete. That is when our partial knowledge becomes full knowledge and I believe we'll see markers on our map that we never noticed before.

The Continuing Mission

Like Magellan's sailors, who carried the voyage home after their captain was gone, I want my family to continue the journey long after I've laid down my maps. To pick up where I left off. To add their own sections. To discover their own landmarks. To navigate their own storms with the compass I helped point them to live by.

My prayers aren't just for my biological family, but my spiritual family too. Those influenced by Young Life involvement, kids I met at camps decades ago who are now adults raising their own children. Those I've worked with in the Air Force, at the Pentagon, at Booz Allen, people who saw faith lived out in ordinary work settings. The church community, relatives, neighbors, and friends that prayed through my illness and whose lives I've witnessed in turn. Other spiritual youth groups who are doing the same faithful work Young Life does. And those who might read these words, strangers I'll never meet but who might find a compass bearing in something I've shared.

The mission is bigger than any individual navigator. It's the mission Jesus gave his disciples:

> Go therefore and make disciples of all nations, baptizing them in the name of the Father and of the Son and of the Holy Spirit, teaching them to observe all that I have commanded you.

> — Matthew 28:19-20

The disciples didn't finish this mission. Paul didn't finish all that he set out to do and neither did Augustine or Luther. None of the great saints and theologians and missionaries finished. They all left unfinished maps. Incomplete work. Unreached people. One day, when the last sailor reaches home, when the last navigator completes the final mile, we'll all be there together to realize we've been part of one great journey home.

The Final Horizon

The ultimate voyage is still ahead. All our maps, all our navigation, all our faithful journeying, it's all pointing toward a destination we haven't reached yet. A horizon we can glimpse but not yet cross.

John wrote about his vision of the future that lies ahead for all who believe.

> And I heard a loud voice from the throne saying, "Look! God's dwelling place is now among the people, and he will dwell with them. They will be his people, and God himself will be with them and be their God. He will wipe every tear from their eyes. There will be no more death or mourning or crying or pain, for the old order of things has passed away."
>
> — Revelation 21:3-4 NIV

Read that again slowly. God's dwelling place will be among the people.

No more tears. Think of every tear you've cried. Every loss. Every grief. Every disappointment. Every wound. God himself will wipe them away. Not dismiss them. Not minimize them. Wipe them away.

No more death. The thing we're all navigating toward, the horizon line we can't avoid, the final storm every sailor must face, it ends. Death itself dies. The last enemy will be defeated.

No more mourning or crying or pain. Everything that makes this voyage hard, everything that makes us long for home, everything that creates the ache we carry, will pass away. The old order, with all its brokenness and struggle and incompleteness, will be gone.

That's the final horizon. That's where every faithful journey leads. That's the destination that makes every incomplete map complete.

Until then, our calling is to keep sailing and navigating the journey we are on as well as to continue preparing those who will come behind us. We're all part of a voyage that started before us and will continue after us, but that will one day reach its glorious destination.

And then we'll all be there together. Every generation. Every faithful navigator. We will stand before the One True North who has been our destination our entire lives.

That's what we're navigating toward. That's the final horizon. That's the destination worth every storm, every struggle, every uncertain step along the way.

And it makes every incomplete map worth drawing.

To My Crew

To Tami, who has navigated beside me for nearly sixty years: Thank you for being my co-navigator, my anchor, my constant reminder of God's faithfulness. Thank you for your laughter, fun spirit, rambunctious attitude, lively conversations, and most of all your patience with me! The maps we've drawn together are our greatest accomplishment.

To our children: You've already exceeded my navigation skills in many ways. Your faith journeys have taught me as much and more than I've taught you. Keep sailing. Keep trusting. Keep passing on what you've learned.

To our grandchildren and great-grandchildren: Some of you I've been able to teach directly, others will have to learn from the maps I've left behind. Know that God has heard every prayer I've prayed for you and every lesson I've learned is available to you, every bit of faith I've accumulated is part of your inheritance.

To those struggling with direction: Your map isn't finished. The storm you're in isn't your final position. The Navigator is still at work, still faithful, still able to guide you home.

Final Encouragement and Commissioning

As I close these pages, I want to remind you: The journey you are on will be finished. Mine will too. That's not pessimism. That's reality. And strangely, it's also freedom.

Some of you reading this have decades of navigation ahead. You're just starting out. The horizon stretches wide before you. The voyage feels endless. You can't imagine the edge of the map approaching.

Others, like me, can see the edge of the map approaching. Not necessarily tomorrow. Maybe not even next year. But it's there. Visible. Real. Closer than it used to be.

But wherever you are in the journey, whatever your age or stage or health or circumstances, the same truth applies: navigate faithfully while you can.

Faithful navigation means checking your bearings regularly. Correcting course when you drift. Trusting True North even when clouds block the stars. Keep going even when you can't see clearly. That's possible. That's the goal.

So live with courage. Not the courage that comes from seeing the whole path laid out clearly before you. Not the courage that comes from having all the answers or knowing exactly what's next. But the courage that comes from knowing the Navigator. From trusting that True North holds even when you can't see it. From believing that God is faithful even when He feels absent.

Train your crew, whether that's your family, your biological children and grandchildren; your friends, the people who walk alongside you through ordinary days; your church community, the body of believers God has placed you among; or people you'll never meet, people who might read your story someday, who might find courage in your example.

Leave behind a map that points to the North Star. Not a map that says, "I was perfect." Not a map that hides the failures or the detours or the times you got completely lost. But a map that honestly shows the journey, mistakes and all, and consistently points back to the One who remained faithful through it all.

And trust that when your part of the voyage is done, others will continue the journey. Your unfinished map will become someone else's starting point. They'll pick up where you left off. They'll add their own discoveries. They'll navigate their own storms using wisdom you helped provide.

Your partial understanding will contribute to someone else's fuller picture. What you learned the hard way might save them from learning it the same way. What you discovered about God's faithfulness will encourage them when their own faith wavers.

Your faithful navigation, however imperfect, will help someone else find their way. Not because you were extraordinary. But because you were faithful. Because you stayed on course. Because you kept True North in view.

The journey continues. It always has. It always will. Until that final day when every map is complete, every navigator arrives home, and we discover that the journey itself was preparing us for a destination more wonderful than we ever imagined.

Until then, keep sailing. Keep checking your bearings. Keep correcting course. Keep trusting True North.

The Navigator is faithful. Even when you doubt. Even when you drift. Even when you fail. He remains faithful. He cannot deny Himself.

The North Star still shines. The clouds may block it. The storm may obscure it. But it's there. Constant. Unchanging. Reliable.

And the crew, your crew, is watching and learning, preparing to carry on when you pass them the wheel. They're seeing how you navigate. They're learning what you trust. They're discovering whether your faith holds under pressure.

What you do now echoes in their future. The map you draw becomes their reference. The compass you follow becomes their guide.

Make it count. Make it faithful. Make it true.

Reflection and Application

Reflect: Who is your "crew"? Who will continue the journey of faith after you? Your children? Your grandchildren? Students you've taught? People you've mentored? Friends you've influenced?

What navigation tools are you leaving for them? What practices? What examples? What wisdom? What stories of God's faithfulness?

How do you believe God (True North) has impacted your life? Where have you seen His faithfulness? When has He proven true even when everything else was uncertain?

ACT: This week, share one spiritual practice, story, or piece of wisdom with someone in your family or community. Add a marker to their map. Don't wait for the perfect moment. Don't wait until you feel wise enough. Just share something true. Something that helped you. Something that might help them.

If you haven't already, consider writing down a few of your own navigation stories. Times when God proved faithful. Lessons learned through failure. Moments when the path became clear. Storms you weathered. Compasses that held true. These stories are gifts. Don't let them die with you.

PRAY: *Lord, thank You that the journey is bigger than me. Thank You for those who navigated before me and left maps for me to follow. For parents and grandparents. For mentors and teachers. For saints and martyrs whose faithfulness lights the way.*

Help me sail faithfully while I can. Not perfectly, but faithfully. Not without mistakes, but without quitting. Not seeing everything clearly, but trusting You.

Prepare my crew to carry the mission forward. Give them courage. Give them wisdom. Give them faith to trust You when their turn comes to navigate.

May the map I leave behind point them to You, my True North. Not to me. Not to my accomplishments or my wisdom. But to You. To Your faithfulness. To Your constant presence.

And thank You for the promise that one day, every journey will be complete in You. Every incomplete map will be finished. Every partial sight will become full sight. Every faithful step will reach its destination.

Until then, help me keep sailing. Amen.

AND ALWAYS REMEMBER: "Be joyful in hope, patient in affliction, and faithful in prayer" (Romans 12:12 NIV).

Joyful in hope, because the destination is sure even when the path is unclear.

Patient in affliction, because storms pass and God remains faithful.

Faithful in prayer, because prayer is the compass that keeps us pointed toward True North.

The journey continues. Your part of it matters. Navigate faithfully.

And trust that when your map is complete, others will pick it up and keep sailing toward that final, glorious horizon where every journey ends and real life begins.

Bibliography

Scripture

All Scripture quotations are taken from the Holy Bible, English Standard Version (ESV), unless otherwise noted. Key passages: Genesis 12:1–4; Numbers 14; Isaiah 53:6; Psalm 23; Psalm 119:105; Proverbs 3:5–6; Matthew 2:1–12; Matthew 4:19; John 16:13; Romans 12:12; Philippians 3:12–14; Hebrews 11:8–10; Hebrews 13:8; Revelation 21:1.

Primary Works and Authors Quoted

Augustine, St. *Confessions*. Translated by Henry Chadwick. Oxford University Press, 1998.

Bonhoeffer, Dietrich. *Life Together*. New York: Harper & Row, 1954.

Merton, Thomas. *New Seeds of Contemplation*. New York: New Directions, 1961.

Nouwen, Henri J. M. *The Return of the Prodigal Son*. New York: Image Books, 1992.

Peterson, Eugene H. *A Long Obedience in the Same Direction*. Downers Grove, IL: Inter-Varsity Press, 1980.

Roosevelt, Theodore. *The Strenuous Life: Essays and Addresses*. New York: The Century Co., 1900.

Shackleton, Ernest. *South: The Story of Shackleton's Last Expedition*. London: Heinemann, 1919.

Smith, William. *A Delineation of the Strata of England and Wales*. London: 1815.

Harrison, John. *The Principles of Mr. Harrison's Timekeeper*. London: 1767.

Historical and Illustrative References

"California as an Island." European Map Series, 1620–1747. British Library, London.

"Columbus's Miscalculation." Library of Congress Historical Collections.

"Wrong Way Corrigan." Smithsonian National Air and Space Museum Archives, 1938.

"GPS Selective Availability Policy History." U.S. Department of Defense, 2000.

"The Longitude Act of 1714." British Parliament Archives.

"Magnetic vs. True North Declination." U.S. Geological Survey (USGS), 2018.

"Sacagawea and the Lewis and Clark Expedition." U.S. National Archives.

Biblical and Theological References

The ESV Study Bible. Wheaton, IL: Crossway, 2008.

The New Bible Commentary. Downers Grove, IL: IVP Academic, 1994.

The NIV Application Commentary Series. Grand Rapids, MI: Zondervan, 1996–2015.

The Anchor Yale Bible Dictionary. Edited by David Noel Freedman. New Haven, CT: Yale University Press, 1992.

Bibliography

Personal and Oral Sources

Gladstone, Thomas, and Tami Gladstone. Personal interviews and correspondence, 2023–2025.

Beckwith, Rick. Foreword to *Finding North in Your Life: A Path to Spiritual Awareness.*

Miller, Jeff B. Co-author interviews and editorial notes, 2024–2025.

Young Life Archives, Fairfax, Virginia, 1970–1990.

Acknowledgments

No book comes to life alone. I want to thank the many people who encouraged, prayed, and supported me throughout the process of writing these pages.

To my Tami, thank you for sixty years of love, patience, and steady support throughout this journey. You have been my constant companion, my rock, my Christ-centered best friend—always reminding me of God's faithfulness, especially when I couldn't see it myself.

To my children, grandchildren, great-grandchild and family, thank you for your encouragement, companionship, love, and prayers. You are the crew I'm preparing, the legacy I'm leaving. Your presence in my life is one of God's greatest gifts.

To Tami's sister Tracey and brother Wayne, and all our close relatives and friends, thank you for cheering me on, sharing wisdom, and reminding me of the bigger picture when I felt stuck. Your friendship has been both a compass and an anchor.

To my church community at Nativity Catholic Church in Burke, Virginia, your prayers, fellowship, and accountability have been a source of strength. You are the body of Christ with hands and feet, and I'm grateful to be part of you.

To my fellow veterans, those I served with and those who may be reading this, thank you for your camaraderie and for giving me inspiration to write these pages. You taught me about courage, faithfulness under fire, and staying on course when everything's chaos.

To our great friend and Young Life companion over the years, Rick Beckwith, thank you for writing the Foreword in this book. Your mentorship, advice, and love for Tami and me during our 40-year Young Life journey have helped to build our relationship with Jesus and brought us closer to God.

I also want to thank Jeff Miller, my co-author. His faithfulness, skill, and dedication shaped these stories into a book that points to Christ. Jeff's work behind the scenes, gathering examples, weaving Scripture, and refining the message, was essential in bringing these pages to life. I am deeply grateful for his partnership in this journey.

Above all, I give thanks to God, whose grace, wisdom, and presence are the true source of every word you will read. Without Him, this would just be one man's memoirs. With Him, it's a map pointing toward something eternal. All glory to Him.